Total Footb Kickstart: A Beginner's Guide and Essential Tips

Anthony E. Martinez

Advantages of Football

Football is much more than just the actual game. It teaches a great deal of knowledge and valuable life lessons. The game has the power to drastically alter someone's physical, mental, social, and emotional well-being. Some people struggle for years or even a lifetime to achieve such priceless objectives. It's never too late to start and join a movement that will benefit your life in many ways.

brain-muscle communication.

The ability to control the muscles and carry out multi-limb operational movements is a function of the central nervous system (CNS). Athletes go through a variety of sessions with varying exercise routines. These exercises are useful for assisting with the muscular system's quick movements and coordination.

helps the brain's cognitive processes.

It has to do with how the mind can take any information and process, store, receive, change, and recover it. Players on the field and coaches must maintain mental stability throughout the game to move through different game plans in order to score goals. A player's mind is constantly searching for territorial advantages or weaknesses of the opposition to gain the upper hand in the game, even while taking breaks.

develops a work ethic.

Football is a game that develops self-discipline because it requires routine behavior.

Sometimes, players are unaware of the amount of effort and dedication necessary to produce a win. Football players must practice every other day besides the day of the game in order to strengthen their weaknesses. Football players have to report to their practice sessions every day because playing the game is their job as athletes, and doing so fosters a strong sense of responsibility.

stable mentality.

Football demands a lot of exercise time, which helps increase strength and maintain a healthy body weight. The player can maintain normal endorphin levels and foster a steady mental state by engaging in such a process. Numerous studies reveal that beginning sports helped people with depression and anxiety cope with their conditions better. It kept them active and helped them feel less stressed.

Concentration.

There is a lot of excitement, noise, and distraction when a game is ongoing. Football players can eventually achieve a mental state of mind that enables them to focus despite the chaos.

Grit.

Nobody can predict how a game will turn out, and sometimes overthinking it can ruin everything. Another thing that many players have learned is the importance of having a strong sense of team spirit and persevering throughout the game (and season).

Quick thinking & Problem-solving.

Football is a fast-paced sport that requires players to make quick decisions. It encourages quick and practical solutions to issues when in the field. For many players, using these mental exercises in a crisis off the field is very helpful.

reduces stress.

It takes a lot of energy and adrenaline rush to play the game, which helps to decompress. Players develop a habit of mental calmness in such an environment and are less likely to experience anxiety or depression.

mood enhancer.

When a player is engaged in the game, their focus and objective unite, focusing all of their energy on the objective. The intensity of the excitement increases before or during the play, squelching any other feelings that might interfere with their game plan. In a way, the game aids in eradicating the blues and promotes optimistic, competitive, and forward-thinking thoughts.

an enjoyable activity.

The exercise is made more enjoyable by the thrill of victory and the team's enthusiasm and support. Every football team has a sense of brotherhood or family that they share as a group, which is helpful when working out and going through the demanding exercise routine. When players train together, there is a spirit of support and inspiration shared, which makes it more enjoyable and motivating.

Teamwork

Football is a true team sport. Each player is expected to play their specific role because there are 11 players on each side of the ball. Each player must be held extremely accountable for performing a specific task on every play. Children learn to collaborate with others through teamwork, a skill that is necessary in almost all occupations.

physical abrasion

Football is one of the most physically demanding sports, along with rugby and hockey. Compared to most other sports, there may be a higher risk of injury, and bruises and bumps are almost a given. The players learn to push through the pain and still give it their all despite any potential limitations as these bumps and bruises eventually heal. This seems to be a metaphor for life, don't you think?

Mental fortitude

Football players must have a strong mind in addition to physical toughness. Children frequently learn mental toughness that they might not have learned otherwise, whether it's overcoming a minor injury or adversity after a turnover or mistake.

Cross-Training

Some young people may already be aware of their preferred sport and may wish to participate in it at a higher level in the future. For those kids, playing football can serve as a fantastic off-season form of cross-training. On the football field, several abilities like hand-eye coordination, a

Contents

PART I

CHARACTERS

We become just by performing just actions, temperate by performing temperate actions, brave by performing brave actions.

—Aristotle

THE EVOLUTION OF URBAN MEYER AND HIS SPREAD OPTION OFFENSE

FALL 2008

The book *Spread Formation Football*, written by Coach Meyer, begins with the line: "Spread formations are not new to football." Very true. Wait, I should have been more specific. *Spread Formation Football* was written in 1952 by Coach Dutch Meyer of Texas Christian University. Yet that Meyer's edict applies with as much force to today's Coach Meyer as it did then, if not more so, and it highlights a simple truth. Urban Meyer and his offensive coordinator at the University of Florida, Dan Mullen, are not geniuses, nor are they innovators. Indeed, Florida's offense is not new; it is not novel; it is not even that unique. Urban Meyer would agree and say that's okay. While his offense may not be new, it is instead something much better—extremely good.

Urban Meyer does not run the wing-t from shotgun (his offense is not based around "series football" as those offenses are); he does not run the run-and-shoot with more running; and the option is only one part of Meyer's offense. Instead, the inspirational fathers of Florida's offense are Joe Gibbs and Dennis Erickson, two coaches who helped establish and pioneer the one-back offense. Indeed, Florida's main run plays are basically the same ones both made popular in the '80s, though from the shotgun and with a bit more option sprinkled in.

Surprised to hear these roots? Meyer is not shy; he admits that he was a late mover to the spread offense. In a time when the newness of the spread has worn off and some spread offenses are awful, we still have Meyer's flying circus, complete with his rhinoceros quarterback, Tim Tebow.

Prior to becoming the head coach at Florida, Urban Meyer bounced around as an assistant coach, finally as receivers coach at Notre Dame under the (surprisingly) schematically brilliant but instinctively Cro-Magnon Bob Davie. In his book, Meyer recalled a moment when, after a loss to Nebraska in 2001, he found one of his best players, David Givens, crying at his locker because he felt he had been unable to help his team win: he hadn't touched the ball the entire game. Meyer then swore to run an offense that delivered the ball to his playmakers. While at Notre Dame, Meyer began meeting with his intellectual mentor, Scott Linehan (his professional mentor was, among others, Lou Holtz). (At the time, Scott Linehan was the offensive coordinator at the University of Louisville; he would later become the offensive coordinator for the Minnesota Vikings, the head coach for the St. Louis Rams, and is currently the offensive coordinator for the Detroit Lions.) Meyer was eventually hired as head coach of Bowling Green and decided that—in years that just happened to be the rather formative ones for the spread offense— he would have his staff learn at these underground masters' feet.

Eschewing typical hotspots like Ohio State, Michigan, and Florida, Meyer directed his staff to make a Midwest pilgrimage to learn from Linehan at Louisville, Joe Tiller and Jim Chaney at Purdue, Randy Walker and Kevin Wilson at Northwestern, and Rich Rodriguez at West Virginia. What they all had in common was that they were one-back or shotgun spread offense coaches and they each had organized, conceptual ways of thinking about football. In short, they were not big names, and many had not even any many championships yet, but as a coach's coach, Meyer could see they were on the cutting edge. So, before Meyer's first season at Bowling Green in 2001, Mullen, Meyer, and the rest of the staff looked to blend the ideas they collected. Over the course of just a handful of weeks, they diagrammed their concepts out, debated them, and converted them to a computer: Meyer's first "spread offense" playbook, which would come to be copied over and over again at every level of football, had been written.

But this is not a story solely about schemes. Meyer has always won football games, wherever he has been. When he arrived at Bowling Green, he engineered one of the great turnarounds in football history; you don't do that with schemes alone, as football history is laden with great schemers who failed to convert ideas into on-field victories.

So what did Meyer actually learn from these programs and coaches? We can see from the coach he eventually became. Broadly, Meyer and his offensive coordinator, Mullen, wanted to be shotgun focused, to spread the field, to throw the football effectively, and to run the ball and run option or quarterback read plays. That hardly narrows it down, but that's the beauty. The simplicity comes in how few schemes are needed to cover all of these bases, and how almost cliché they are in practice: the inside and outside zones and the zone read, the counter, the trap, the quarterback power, and the option game (with jet or speed sweeps sprinkled in, just to get speedy players to the perimeter). This is the same spread offense playbook high school teams are running; indeed, there's little that Meyer runs now that Northwestern and West Virginia weren't running back then. Most of the differences are cosmetic.

Meyer learned his passing offense primarily from what Purdue and Louisville were doing in their spread heydays, though it is important to note that both Purdue and Louisville at the time were traditional one-back spread offenses but with more shotgun, so although Meyer focused on their passing games, their running games were consistent with the spread run game Meyer was installing. But the defining feature of Meyer's offense is not his passing game, it's the running game. And that is all based around simple arithmetic.

Indeed, more important than the actual concepts Meyer uses is his approach. Although his quarterback is a run threat, Meyer's offense is not analogous to traditional triple option teams. This is because Meyer's offense—like most other spreads—is not entirely based around series football, or a set play followed by its counter followed by the counter to the counter. Instead it is a more conceptual, more pro- or NFL-style approach.

The entire theory can be summarized briefly: if the defense plays with two safeties back—so long as the offense forces the defense to cover its receivers by employing constraint plays like bubble screens—the offense has a numbers advantage up front to run the ball. Think about it: there are eleven players on both sides, and the defense always has one counterpart for the ball carrier. But if the quarterback is a threat to run the ball—and he doesn't have to be great at it, just a threat—the defense will lack sufficient numbers to deal with the players the offense has that can run with the ball, block, or fake running the ball (the quarterback), if the defense keeps two defenders deep *and* covers all of the split wide receivers. This last part is the key: it is the role the bubble screens and other constraint plays have on the defense.

But if the defense plays with a single-deep defender there is no advantage in the box, but the offense should be able to pass, as it does have enough numbers to protect the quarterback and the receivers should be in (effectively) one-on-one situations. So a team like Florida will likely throw the ball. Against soft coverage, the offense will look to throw underneath; against press or tight coverage, the offense will play around with the receivers' alignments to free them up for downfield or quick outside throws.

Finally, if there is no deep safety then the offense knows the defense is in Cover 0 and it therefore expects the defense to blitz. The defense is saying either we're going to get you, or you're going to get a big play; we're betting on us. Florida has a lot of responses, but at some point you have to be willing to go deep against Cover 0.

That's really it. From there, Meyer looks to individual matchups or slight structural or leverage advantages. So long as the defense stays in its base defense, Meyer and Mullen run their base plays and it's just about execution. And soon as defenders get out of position or try to get cute, Meyer and company go to their constraint plays.

During coaching clinics, Meyer often mentions that he likes to ask defensive coaches what they hate to defend, and he says their answer is always option football. The most famous "spread option" play, the zone read—in which the quarterback reads an unblocked backside defender to decide whether to keep the ball or hand it to a running back—is not truly option football: it's a nice wrinkle, but it is not designed in such a way that the offense is correct every time. The reason is because the initial read is of the backside defensive end; if he stays put, the success of the play is contingent on however the blocks on the play side turn out. On a true front side triple option play, however, the play should essentially work so long as the reads are correct. The zone read is instead an improved bootleg: it keeps the defense honest against the base runs, but that is it.

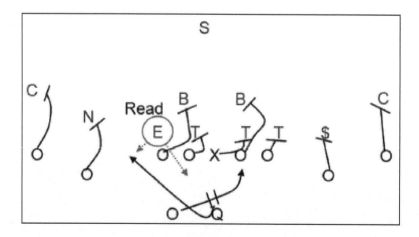

But Florida has increasingly used forms of *true* option football. One variant is the veer: the way Meyer uses it, it's a double, not a triple option, but if Tim Tebow reads it correctly (which is not always his strength), the play is almost certain to work because both the blocking and the read itself go to the same side. On the play, the offensive line—say, to the right—ignores certain defensive linemen while going on to block different defenders downfield. The running back heads inside of the defender being read; if he fails to react to the running back, it's an easy handoff. If he does try to tackle that running back, then the quarterback simply steps around him for what is often a big gain.

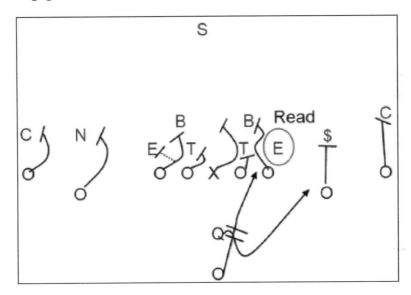

So the offense gets a good deal: it gets double teams it would not have otherwise gotten by "blocking" defenders through optioning off of them. While option football is not easy, you have a better chance of success optioning off a great defensive end to make him wrong rather than trying to have an overmatched tight end or fullback try to block them.

Moreover, Florida also commonly uses its shovel triple option, where Tebow attacks an unblocked defender with an option to either side of him: a running back or tight end to the inside so Tebow can "shovel" or flip the ball forward, or another to his outside in a traditional speed option look to receive a pitch. The purpose of the play is to get the ball to the shovel player inside of the hard charging defense, but when run properly, the defense should always be wrong inside or outside, every time. This is the beauty of the spread: the options are nearly endless.

How might you defend this offense? It's not difficult—in theory. And, clearly, teams have gotten better at defending such spread looks as more and more teams have been using them. But defending a team like Florida, with all their talent—Tebow, Percy Harvin and Aaron Hernandez, to name just a few of Meyer's weapons—is quite the chore. And if the quarterback can run, the offense gains the advantage of an additional threat.

Against the old option attacks, the quarterback's counterpart had to line up on the line of scrimmage and hit the quarterback near the line, and thus the defense had to play essentially without a deep safety. Against the I-formation attacks so popular in the '90s, the quarterback's counterpart—the free safety—could stand back in the middle of the field and keep the quarterback from throwing against single coverage. Indeed, the rage in the '90s was the rise of the eight-man front defense, which the spread developed to counter.

But against the spread where the quarterback is a legitimate dual threat, like Florida with their Heisman winner, the defense must do *both* of these elements. The quarterback's counterpart has to be on the line of scrimmage to hit the quarterback on runs (as with the option attacks) while he must also be back in the middle against passes. This is not a debatable point; it is arithmetic, not theory. And it proves that while Meyer's offense is simple to defend, it is not easy.

The answer is that you have to have safety-type players who can play the quarterback but also can, if it is a pass play, race back and play as either an intermediate defender or as a deep safety. The defense must be able to play man coverage, and it must have the ability to blitz and attack both the quarterback and any other backfield player. Finally, the defense must have the ability to zone blitz to put pressure on the quarterback but still take away the short slants and quick passes, or at least threaten to be able to do so.

In other words, you have to play defense like Alabama head coach Nick Saban. But there is no foolproof system; speed is king; and players win games. And there is no doubt that a spread offense like Florida's is beautiful to watch because it forces the defense to play perfectly; to succeed, the opposing defense must be able to multitask like never before.

Woody Hayes, Ohio State's legendary former coach, built his defenses around his understanding of the converse of the principle behind the spread offense. An autodidact of military history and strategy, Hayes understood that the best and simplest way to stop an offense's attack was to corral it into a controllable space, as small as possible, to limit its available strategies. Having done that, you could then predict your opponent's methods of attack and close them off. Meyer's offense—like all good spread offenses—seeks to flip the advantage back to the offense by stretching the defense from sideline to sideline.

But let's go one step further. Why does that work, particularly with regard to the run game? You hear about the benefits of the spread offense from sportscasters with little explanation of why (other than vague generalizations or incorrect statements about "one-on-one matchups"). The answer is that, executed correctly, spreading your formation to run gives you something far more valuable than a one-on-one matchup: leverage. Meyer's schemes are not tricky, nor are they original. But they are sound. When you block a front, you do not send your linemen—however big and however talented—to just fly out to hit a defender to try, in a hopeless attempt, to make the defender go where he does not want to. Instead, you put your kids in position to win. You use double-teams. You trap defenders who rush hard upfield. And you option off of defenders to make them wrong, every time. Football is still a game about power, strength, and quickness, but it's always better to be smart about how to focus that power, strength, and quickness where it is most likely to be successful.

If the old running offenses of yesteryear, in reflecting earlier times, were like punishing boxers who engaged in matches where the biggest and strongest won, then offenses like Meyer's and the other teams that showcase the best of the spread, in reflecting their times, are like martial arts: without sacrificing either strength or power, they punish you but also use speed, quickness, and cleverness to hit you where you do not expect, always probing to find your weak spots, and to exploit them, without mercy.

THE 3-3-5 DEFENSE: A STORY OF INNOVATION (AND DESPERATION)

FALL 2009

The modern 3–3–5 defense (also known as the "3–5–3" or "30 stack") is a defense of relatively recent vintage. Maybe most famously, Rich Rodriguez and his defensive coordinator at West Virginia, Jeff Casteel, used it with success, but the defense developed in basically three places: South Carolina under defensive coordinator and now Louisville head coach Charlie Strong, Mississippi State (under defensive coordinator Joe Lee Dunn), and Georgia Military College.

New ideas in football tend to arise as potential solutions to specific problems. And, in early 2000, Charlie Strong and Lou Holtz had a serious problem. They had gone to South Carolina promising big results but had, instead, finished an abysmal 0–11 (South Carolina had gone 1–10 the previous season). That first season Strong had little luck defending talented SEC squads with a depleted roster arranged solely in traditional defensive alignments. Holtz and Strong therefore needed something novel, multiple, and, above all else, functional to combat superior foes. The answer was the 3–3–5 defense, a defense with three down linemen, three true linebackers stacked behind those linemen, and five defensive backs—three in the traditional mold and two hybrid strong safeties/outside linebackers to patrol the flats, blitz, and cover tight ends and slots. The result? In 2000, with its revamped defense (along with a revamped shotgun spread offense to go with it), South Carolina went 8–4—including 5–3 in the SEC—and defeated Ohio State in the Outback Bowl. But the 3–3–5 didn't just occur to Charlie Strong out of the blue; it was a natural variant from the defense he coached in another venue under Holtz: Bob Davie's 3–4 defenses at Notre Dame.

Strong came to South Bend as a position coach under Lou Holtz, but he also coached under Bob Davie, who first was the Irish's defensive coordinator and later became its head coach. Although no one will confuse Davie with Bear Bryant or Paul Brown on a list of football coaching legends, he did coach some great defenses—unfortunately for him, many were at Texas A&M, before he became the head coach of Notre Dame. Indeed, within coaching circles he is widely credited with stopping—or at least severely hampering—the rise of the famed run-and-shoot offense that made David Klinger and Andre Ware famous at the University of Houston. To battle the four-wide all-the-time run-and-shoot (a predecessor to today's ubiquitous spread attacks), Davie devised a series of blitzes that set off a chain reaction of problems for Houston's offense: Davie forced Houston to keep its running back in to pass protect, thus keeping him out of the pass pattern; at the same time, his defense remained in a simple, deep zone coverage; and, despite all this, he was able to free an unblocked pass rusher—as the wily former Bears and Eagles coach Buddy Ryan used to say, no quarterback ever completed a pass while flat on his back. Indeed, against Davie's Texas A&M defenses in the early 1990s, the Cougars' offense—which at some points had averaged more than fifty or sixty points a game—was beaten up and confused, and to many (rightly or wrongly), the 'shoot's sparkle forever dimmed.

Davie did all this out of a 3–4 front (three defensive linemen and four linebackers) with a heavy focus on zone blitzing, as is common with most 3–4 teams. Although much discussed, zone blitzing is not particularly well understood, and it is key to any 3–3 defense. Zone blitzes do not always involve a lineman dropping into coverage (though sometimes they do), and it is not an all-out blitz—in fact, it is the opposite. Instead, a zone blitz is any defensive scheme that rushes at least five but usually not more than six players, where behind that pass rush the defense plays zone coverage. That's it. That simple framework, however, presents offenses with a number of problems.

Historically, blitzes required man coverage. This was a matter of arithmetic: if you blitz a few extra players you don't have enough defenders to cover all the zones, so you must use man coverage. Thus, offenses began using hot routes—passes that could be completed quickly before a blitzer could arrive—like slants and quick shallow crosses, which, for decades, could be audibled to or sight adjusted to on the fly whenever the defense showed a man-to-man blitz. When defenses began zone blitzing in earnest, however, the quarterback's hot reads were suddenly all wrong: instead of throwing a slant away from the man defender for a big play, the ball would land in the chest of a zone defender who had dropped from the interior or flowed from the opposite side. Or the quarterback would look for his hot read and—realizing a defender was in the way—freeze up, thus allowing the pocket to collapse around him for a sack. Confusion reigned.

And, because a zone blitz only involves five or maybe six pass rushers, the defense is not simply trying to bring more than the offense can block. Instead, it tries to be smart in how it attacks the offense's protection schemes. Part of this is technique: the reason you see linemen backing off so often is because the defense can get a two for one—the defensive lineman drops into coverage and the offensive linemen, thinking the defender is going to pass rush, steps toward him, and by the time the blocker figures out that someone else is rushing, he can't get over to make a block and has actually failed to block anyone at all. (Linebackers too can do this by lining up on the line and taking a step forward like they plan to blitz before backing out.) The other way zone blitzes break down protections is schematic: defensive coaches work to figure out how best to deploy those five rushers to get the holy grail of blitzing—the free, unblocked rusher.

The most common zone blitz tactic is a fire zone, which uses a three-deep, three-under coverage approach, though zone blitzes with two-deep and four defenders underneath are not uncommon. The deep defenders play deep just as you would imagine (with some additional technique, of course), while the underneath or intermediate zone defenders typically use pattern read or matchup zone principles—they study your schemes and play man on you while you're in their zone by anticipating the offense's route combinations. In short, while they play zone they don't just defend areas but actually defend receiver routes. Generally, the coverage in a zone blitz is intended to neither give up the easy play nor the big one and to let the well-designed blitz get to the quarterback or running back. All-out man-to-man blitzes, on the other hand, are typically designed to get to the quarterback—or else. So, against a zone blitz, if an offense can protect its quarterback, it can find big windows between the zones. But that's a big if, and, even if successful, the zone blitz is not likely to give up an immediate touchdown as a man blitz might.

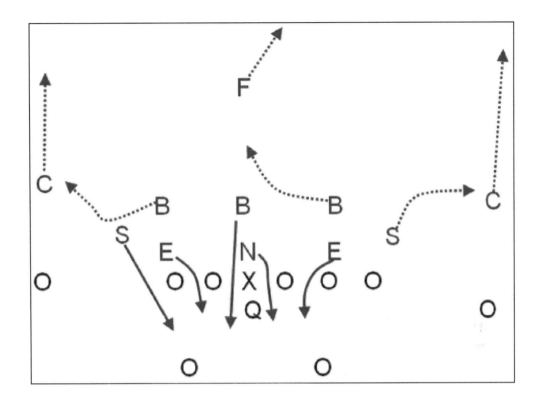

All these were lessons Davie's success on defense reinforced for Charlie Strong and which Strong later used in his 3–3–5 at South Carolina. For Strong, the 3–3–5 was just Bob Davie's disrupting 3–4 mixed with some of the newest and best of the NFL's defenses—essentially an all-the-time nickel package—designed to be run by a team in South Carolina that simply didn't have the personnel to throw an extra linebacker in there and so would benefit from stacking its linebackers behind defensive linemen to keep them hidden and away from blockers.

At this time in the early 2000s, all of college football—and, really, every level of football—was in the midst of a grand upheaval as the spread offense forced changes on defense: the trend was speed, and there was no sign of abatement. Gone were the conservative matches of brute strength exemplified in the days of

Woody Hayes; change had come, and it could only be met with more change.

Though there are different 3–3 styles, Strong's was of the attacking variety. As he told cavtalk.20m.com at the time: "What we like to do is disrupt offenses. We want to disrupt, and we want to set the tempo for the game. We feel like if we do that, we always have a chance." On just about every snap, his linemen were instructed to attack a gap—the space between offensive linemen—and to get into the backfield and make things generally unpleasant for offenses. The 3–3–5 is designed to make both pass protection and run schemes, particularly zone-blocking schemes that heavily rely on double-team blocks, difficult to the point of futility. The linebackers have varying assignments, from blitz to coverage, but they too are responsible for gaps. One important benefit of this is that it simplifies assignments for players: attack your gap and make a play. But it also puts a lot on the coaches to get the calls right. Being "aggressive" might be a nice buzzword that implies a roving, attacking defense, but if that's all it means, then you're going to lose a lot of games; it has to be done intelligently.

This is an important difference between the 3–3–5 and the 3–4. The traditional 3–4 is a two-gap defense: the defensive linemen typically line up "heads up" on the offensive linemen and are responsible for the gaps on their side of them, while the linebackers are generally free to roam. In the 3–3–5, by contrast, there are more stunts, and usually at least one linebacker is rushing, so each ends up responsible for one specific gap, though (unlike many 4–3 defenses) the player's responsibility will change from play to play.

The attacking 3–3 thus utilizes a kind of intelligent chaos principle: players are told to attack gaps, stunt, blitz, and "fly around and play football," but each call has a reason; every blitz, after taking account of the players' assignments and movements, should put the defense in a tried-and-true front designed to stop specific offensive concepts. So if a 3–3–5 coach calls an overload blitz to one side or tells the defensive line to slant one way or the other, it's because the staff has crunched the numbers and knows that—to use fictitious numbers—87.6 percent of the time out of this or that formation on some particular down the offense runs that direction. Put another way, this isn't about aggressiveness at all; it's about creating new defensive fronts where the players are realigned, after the snap, in a way that sets a trap for the offense to run right into. It's intelligent chaos.

Yet despite the shifting and aggressiveness, the 3–3–5 is, at core, a balanced defense. Equal numbers of defenders align on each side of the ball and typically only one defender must move to account for an extra receiver or blocker to one side or the other. The defense is not perfect and has weaknesses, of course. Charlie Strong did not use the 3–3–5 as any more than a situational package as defensive coordinator at Florida and takes the same approach as head coach of Louisville. But the defense was sound then and remains so.

Though Charlie Strong may have devised his own brand of the 3–3–5 at South Carolina, there was some precedent. Joe Lee Dunn is widely credited as inventing the scheme, first at Memphis and later making it famous at Mississippi State in the mid-1990s. (Currently, Dunn coaches at McMurry University, a Division III school.)

Under Dunn, the 3–3–5 opened to a splash. Scheduled to play Southern Cal in the fall of 1991, Dunn, then Memphis's defensive coordinator—who only two years before had been a graduate assistant—knew he needed something different for his Tigers to have any chance at victory. He also knew he didn't have enough defensive linemen to successfully defend the Trojans. So he swapped out one of his defensive linemen in his traditional 4–3–4 set, made him a defensive back, and the 3–3–5 was born. He shifted the alignments around—lining up the defensive linemen in the way now custom for the 3–3–5, with a nose tackle over the center rather than over an offensive guard as with a 4–3. And it worked: on September 2, 1991, Memphis upset Southern Cal 21–

10. Within a few years, Dunn was an SEC coach, first during three seasons at Ole Miss, then one at Arkansas, before he finally landed on Jackie Sherrill's staff at Mississippi State.

At State, Dunn's defenses were, at least for a time, among the best in the country. They recruited for speed, often from the junior college ranks, and it was the consensus of every coach in the SEC that Dunn's defense was one of the toughest to deal with, in no small part because of its confusing nature. As Nebraska coach Bo Pellini would later say of Dunn's defense during a press conference, "It's unusual; we really don't know what they're going to do," adding, "They've done some unusual things. There is a lot to prepare for."

And at State, Dunn went whole hog with the 3–3–5: almost every game, each defensive player blitzed at least once—and often much more often. Dunn had no fears about locking down defenders in press man coverage one-on-one, and he even sometimes overloaded one side of the offense with seven or even eight defenders just to that side. As with the 3–4, the 3–3–5 defense can make free use of zone blitzes without having to drop a defensive lineman into coverage, unlike with a traditional 4–3. And there is more speed on defense to play around with; more guys who can blitz, fill gaps, or cover, thus giving the defense more options.

Of course, Dunn's career can be a warning about the 3–3–5: he has bounced around, having held down jobs with good schools, but never was able to break out beyond schools like Memphis, Mississippi State, and Ole Miss. And while at its best those defenses were incredibly suffocating, when the talent dropped off, what had been simply aggressiveness seemed to bleed over into over aggressiveness and a penchant for giving up big plays. And since then, he has coached at Ridgeway High School, New Mexico State, and now McMurry in Division III. But Dunn's legacy is secure. He is essentially the father of the 3–3–5, and the teams that now use it are his descendants.

One of those descendants is Georgia Military College, a junior college in Milledgeville, Georgia, that gives out degrees in military science. Obviously out of the public eye, since 2000 GMC has won an NCAA junior college national championship and been runner up twice. 2000 also happens to be when GMC adopted the 3–3–5 defense. In 2001, their first year in the system—installed after meeting with Charlie Strong and Joe Lee Dunn—GMC's defense gave up a mere 67.6 yards per game of total offense.

Yet while Dunn has bounced around from school to school and Strong abandoned the 3–3–5 at Florida as a base defense, GMC, along with a few other schools like the Air Force Academy, have essentially worked out the kinks over the years. They've seen it all: spread, power, multiple tight ends, wing-t sets, options, and so on, each thrown at them in an effort to counteract their confusing "stacked" defense. GMC provides a good example of the kinds of choices a 3–3–5 team has to face.

First is the question of how aggressive and variable the fronts—the arrangement of those three defensive linemen and three linebackers—should be. The best 3–3–5 teams have counteracted their speed-over-size deficit by being multiple, thus dictating the offense's reactions. The most important example of this is in the run game. If you're as multiple as most 3–3–5 coaches are, the offense is commonly forced to stick with zone-blocking schemes, as opposed to specific "I-will-block-him" man-blocking schemes, because otherwise there will be too much confusion about who to block. And, while zone-blocking schemes are very sound, knowledge is half the battle and that allows the defense to focus its preparation.

Second, 3–3–5 teams are infamous for their "prowling": the constant shuffling and movement of defensive players sideways or into and out of gaps before the ball is snapped for play. The idea is that such movement generates confusion for the offense and, when correctly executed (and with the proper attitude), the sight of large, angry defenders threatening to attack from every conceivable angle is its own form of psychological warfare. But sometimes prowling can get defenders out of position: though he is given freedom to move around before the snap, each defender must nevertheless be in position to handle *his* job before each play. This is why, despite the confusion and intimidation factors, some coaches prefer that their defenders simply line up where they are supposed to and leave it at that. Different 3–3–5 teams—as is the case with most defenses, nowadays—have to decide for themselves what works best.

Third, defenses, like everything else in football, can only play as well as their players play. While the goal of any 3–3–5 defense is to play aggressively, attack gaps, and get into the backfield, that only works if the specific defenders have the talent and ability to do it, all while reading the offense. All the stunting in the world won't help if defenders can't "read on the run" as required in a stunting defense.

Finally, this defense tends to put a lot of pressure on the cornerbacks, both in man coverage and in zone coverage which is effectively like man coverage, with very little help. Disguise and movement help 3–3–5 teams cover up flaws, but this does not change the fact that this defense puts its corners—and its primary deep safety—in a lot of open space with a lot of green grass to cover.

The 3–3–5 is certainly no longer the defense of the future, as many of its leading practitioners like Charlie Strong have moved on to other fronts and use it as only a subpackage. But the principles underlying the 3–3–5 remain as relevant as ever: movement, disguise, aggressiveness, and an extreme focus on speed. Those will never go away.

THE ODYSSEY:
A REVIEW OF MIKE LEACH'S
SWING YOUR SWORD

FALL 2011

My first experience with Mike Leach came during a film study session at the University of Kentucky. It was a camp for high school quarterbacks, of which I was one, though I wasn't one of the players they were heavily recruiting. The coaches—particularly head coach Hal Mumme and his recruiting coordinator, Claude Bassett, who would later be banned from college football by the NCAA for recruiting violations—focused most of their attention on Jared Lorenzen, who would later start four years at Kentucky (though only one for Mumme) before bouncing around the NFL. But the camp was a small one, much smaller than your typical college camp, and the Kentucky coaches didn't farm you off to local high school coaches like too many of the big name college camps did then and still do. And the film instructor was some wide receivers coach —"Hey, where is Coach Mumme?"—named Coach Leach.

To make matters worse, we watched the same play, a flood route everyone has in their playbook (he just called it "94"), over and over again against every SEC team they ran it against. And then we got a quiz. "How far is this throw here?" he asked, as he pointed to the ten-yard out. As the route had a "10" next to it to show where the break point was, one hapless soul raised his hand and offered, "Ten yards?" I didn't know where this was going, but I knew that wasn't the right answer, and Coach Leach simply made a face like someone had broken some serious wind.

But he didn't miss a beat and moved onto the next question: "Hey, how many of you remember the Pythagorean theorem?" No one was going to answer that question in a room full of football players, and certainly not after the last offering. "Okay, how many of you guys took geometry?" I sheepishly raised my hand, as did Lorenzen and a couple of others. Most did not. We clearly were a lame audience, so our teacher decided to push us along a little bit more quickly.

"Fine. The deal is that you can figure out how long these throws are using the Pythagorean theorem," he said, as the light went off in my head (oh, yeah, *that* Pythagorean theorem). He quickly showed us how to calculate how far each throw was based on the quarterback's drop, the depth of the route, and how far it was from the quarterback and how close to the sideline. And then we were on to another pass play.

This Mike Leach—analytical, odd (especially in a football context), but ultimately incisive and creative—shines through in his new book, *Swing Your Sword*. The book, edited by Bruce Feldman, formerly of ESPN, is a highly enjoyable look at the former Red Raider coach's upbringing, influences, and experiences as a coach on the fringe who made it to the big leagues, and then suddenly went from the highest of highs (upsetting #1 ranked Texas in November on national television) to being dismissed from his position and finding himself unemployed in the midst of a massive battle with his former employer, Texas Tech, as well as ESPN and ESPN personality Craig James.

But the James fiasco aside, Leach's legacy for those of us into football strategy is as a pass-first maven who, along with Hal Mumme, created the Air Raid offense, an offense that completely took over the high school landscape and won Leach a lot of games (not to mention fans) during his times at Kentucky, Oklahoma, and, most significantly, Texas Tech. The book does a nice job showing how Leach became the kind of coach he would become, as he was particularly drawn to the passing game. It's actually a bit hard to remember now, but for most of football history, if you were a "throwing coach" you were considered more of a trickster than a real coach. Leach says that when he and Mumme got to Valdosta State in Valdosta, Georgia, in the early 1990s, he was often approached by enthusiastic and supportive but concerned fans: "Sometimes people would come up to me at the coffee shop and say, 'I hope you guys do well, but you know you're gonna have to run the ball up the middle here.'"

Leach would respond with niceties before giving up and telling them that "the definition of insanity is doing the same thing over and over again and expecting a different result." This is the Mike Leach that is so appealing: unique, independent of thought but determined. And this charming book does a nice job of explaining how he got that way: how the kid who figured out that the way to get a neighborhood dog to stop peeing on his sleeping bag was to literally pee on the dog became the head coach of a Big 12 school whose teams routinely shattered the record books week in and week out. Unlike most coaching books, you do get a sense for how the coach thinks and how his influences helped him approach the practical problems inherent in coaching football. As Leach puts it:

> Law school helped me in ways I could never have imagined as I was making the transition from law to coaching football. During my first orientation at Pepperdine, one of the professors said that as a law student, you won't be getting a degree in case memorization or rule memorization. Instead, you learn how to take a variety of facts and a certain amount of precedent, and apply them to the problem at hand. You are actually getting a degree in problem solving. Well, football certainly supplies a lot of problems to solve.
>
> As a football coach you begin every week with a fairly sizable problem: how to beat the next opponent. You have a ton of material at your disposal—statistical breakdowns, game film, scouting reports, and you have to prioritize what you're going to delve into, because there's not nearly enough time to cover everything. You choose what to worry about, what to set aside, and what to feature. Then,

ready or not, the game comes, and it's off you go. In the thick of it you have to think on your feet, adapt, and be ready for surprises.

The book also does a nice job meshing Leach's oddball character and history with a more familiar but lesser understood story: a coach's life, which is not an easy one. This kind of story has become something of a cliché, but if it has it remains an honest one. Breaking into coaching is difficult and humbling, and Leach's early career step of getting a job for $3,000 a year and having to substitute teach in the summers is told briskly but well. (Leach tells his wife his new job pays $3,000. She tells him that will be a nice monthly salary. He sheepishly has to explain that it's the *yearly* salary.)

Of course, what *I* wanted to know from this book was where that wonderful offense came from. Although I didn't learn anything particularly new, I did pick up a few details and was able to put the timeline together a bit better. For example, it was interesting to learn that Mumme and Leach cut their offense in half while at Iowa Wesleyan in the very early 1990s, and it wasn't until their second season at Valdosta State that they went with the modern Air Raid set where they permanently aligned the *Y* receiver (which had traditionally been a tight end in a pro set) to the right and the *X* receiver (the split end) to the left and stopped worrying about whether or not the offense was symmetrical. But it was just as fun to read about the zeitgeist surrounding the development of the offense during a time when to be willing to throw it around like they were put them, in the minds of most outsiders, in a spot somewhere between insane and stupid.

[While coaching at Iowa Wesleyan,] Hal and I used to go drink coffee at Dickie's Prairie Home. We'd sit there and talk X's and O's for hours, drawing up plays on napkins...

We tweaked a lot of BYU plays, where we'd change a receiver's route on a given play because we believed it would be more effective. Hal and I would sit there for hours: "If they're in zone (coverage) and we do this, where's the space gonna be?...Are they gonna be more vulnerable here or here?...If we do this, what depth do we want the receiver to be at? Because the quarterback will read this and he'll need to be right around here."

We got ideas from almost every direction we turned. We ran a lot of crossing routes that were similar to what BYU was doing. Not many teams were using crossing routes. I really like them. It's not an incredibly long throw for the quarterback to make. More importantly, defenders can get lost in transition as they're chasing their receivers, making decisions difficult about which receiver is getting passed on to which defender. It's pretty disruptive. Give a defender cause for indecision and you just made him play slow. You can have the greatest technique, and all of the strength and speed in the world, but those things are negated if you hesitate. When a guy hesitates, it can be as bad as busting a play.

One of the fascinating sections of the book was Leach's discussion of the development of his offense at Texas Tech, particularly the "6" route, which is what Mike called his four verticals concept, where four receivers ran down the field to specified landmarks to horizontally stretch the deep coverage. Four verticals has always been in the Air Raid playbook but it hadn't really been exploited as anything more than a way for everyone to run deep until Leach's third season at Texas Tech:

A turning point for us came in my third season at Tech… We got to thinking about all of this space we weren't utilizing. Why weren't we using it?…Run or pass, it's a constant effort to best utilize the space on the field…In the first couple of days of camp, we decided to throw verticals all the time. The first day we completed about 30 percent and I said, "That's bad. We need to do a better job of getting on the same page and this is something we really need to look at." So we talked about it. "If he's open here, you need to throw it. If he's open now, you need to look. You guys aren't on the same page, but we need to get on the same page because there's space everywhere."

The receiver runs the route and looks to the quarterback as the defender adjusts. The receiver keeps running. The quarterback decides when and where to throw the ball. On the throw, the receiver adjusts to the ball. If the receiver stops or settles because he guesses, then he is wrong. If the ball is thrown to the wrong place, where there is no space, then the quarterback is wrong. Where the ball is caught is based upon how the defender chooses to play the route. Simply stated: Throw it where they are not. The execution of this requires months and even years of practice. However, the space is always there, and it's impossible for the defense to cover.

In [quarterback] Kliff [Kingsbury]'s first two seasons as a starter, he averaged 23 TD passes and around 3,450 passing yards. His third season, after we changed our approach on "6," he threw for 41 TDs and 4,500 passing yards.

I've long said that this was when the offense became Leach's offense and not simply Mike Leach running the Air Raid. And if Kingsbury's senior season was the turning point, then the full-blown arrival of the nouveau Leach Air Raid was the next season with a one-year wonder (the first of several under Leach) named B. J. Symons:

> B. J. Symons, the quarterback who took over after Kliff went to the NFL, had a different attitude altogether. He'd say, 'Screw that,' and he'd fire it in—the receiver had better be ready. B. J. didn't care. He'd throw a laser shot and hit the guy in the side of the helmet if he wasn't looking. During the season, he put on a clinic running '6.' He broke Ty Detmer's record for most passing yards in a 12-game season. He broke Kliff's Big 12 record for single-season touchdown passes (52). When we went to Ole Miss to play the Rebels, he upstaged Eli Manning, who is a great quarterback. B. J. threw for 661 yards and we beat them 49–45.

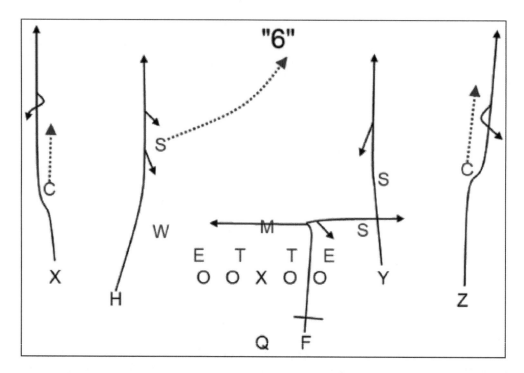

The adjustments to four verticals were certainly crucial to the explosion in Leach's offense, but he doesn't fully bring out that it was a necessary evolution from where he'd brought the offense. At

Kentucky, the Air Raid was primarily a two-back offense; they even ran some traditional play action and offset-I sets. For example, Leach cites as maybe his favorite game from his time at Kentucky as their win over LSU in Baton Rouge, one of the toughest places to play. Against LSU, Mumme and Leach ran the old Air Raid favorites —Y-stick, Y-cross, Mesh—from primarily two running back sets, in a more traditional West Coast offense approach. At Texas Tech, however, Leach used four-wide receivers almost all of the time—true spread-and-shred. Some of this was because of Leach's natural inclinations but a lot of it was the simple fact that his slot receiver— the replacement for the second running back in the offense, the *H*— was Wes Welker, who, despite being essentially unrecruited, turned out to be pretty good at the whole slot receiver thing. Indeed, a lot of the evolution of Leach's offense at Tech was designed around ways to play to Welker's strengths, whether it was running stick concepts to his side as well as the other or using four verticals with an immediate read element to play to his natural ability to find creases in the defense wherever they were.

And this is not an uncommon theme in football: great players often do as much to make the game evolve (from both protagonist as well as antagonist perspectives) as coaches. And the great leap forward for Texas Tech and Leach in 2002–03 was largely sparked by a happenstance combination of this read-on-the-run four verticals plus Wes Welker plus Mike Leach: it was the perfect marriage of the greatest backyard play in football (get open) with one of the greatest backyard players of all time in Welker with maybe the greatest backyard coach to ever roam an actual, honest-to-god Division I sideline.

Oh, and 6? It also happened to be the route Leach called for the famous game winner of Graham Harrell to Michael Crabtree to beat Texas. In that game, Texas Tech went nine of eleven for 173 yards on the 6 play call. Leach says his only regret was he didn't call the play another ten times.

Of course, there are some downsides to Leach's personality which the book doesn't really hide but also doesn't play up. It's clear —more clear to me than before I'd read the book—that Leach really enjoys the limelight, despite his claims to the contrary. During law school he was a wannabe actor (including getting a nonspeaking role as an FBI agent in a J. Edgar Hoover movie), fought with the media departments at Iowa Wesleyan and Valdosta because he wanted to run PR from his office (though he very likely had a point), and clearly relished media attention from noted author Michael Lewis and *60 Minutes*. Now, there's nothing wrong with a little vanity and wanting to be recognized, but when you're Mike Leach you always have to worry about whether or not you've stopped being Mike Leach and started to become the character of Mike Leach. I can't really judge, but it certainly seemed like things had begun to fray for him the end of his tenure at Texas Tech, with the media being a wedge issue between him and his school and possibly even his team. And, of course, the final chapter is, necessarily I suppose, about the Adam James saga that cost him his job. I understand why that chapter is there, but that's not what interests me about Leach.

Undoubtedly Mike will get the opportunity to coach again. Leach was and remains worth studying, both for his successes and also for the things that didn't quite work out. Hopefully he gets back into coaching and puts the distractions behind him so we can see him call 6 a few more times.

Postscript: Leach was hired in late 2011 as the new coach of Washington State.

GARY KUBIAK, ALEX GIBBS, AND THE GREATEST RUN PLAY IN MODERN FOOTBALL

FALL 2011

The good news: you're Gary Kubiak, coach of the Houston Texans, and you will be hosting your first playoff game Saturday. Your opponents are the very beatable 9–7 Cincinnati Bengals. Now, the bad news: your quarterback will likely be T. J. Yates (oh, no!), unless he's hurt, in which case it will be Jake Delhomme (holy crap!), and if both of them are injured, it will be Jeff Garcia ("Fearfulness and trembling are come upon me, and horror hath overwhelmed me," Psalm 55:5). This is Kubiak's dilemma, as he and the Texans have backed into the playoffs after season-ending injuries to starter Matt Schaub and backup Matt Leinart.

Fortunately, unlike most NFL coaches, Kubiak did not build the Texans offense solely around his quarterback. Kubiak, a former assistant under Mike Shanahan with the 49ers and Denver, employs the same West Coast offense passing game that Shanahan used in San Francisco. The foundation of the Texans offense, however, is a running game that has roots in a later iteration of the Kubiak/Shanahan collaboration—the late 1990s Denver Broncos.

When Shanahan went to Denver in 1995, he brought his West Coast passing plays with him and enlisted Kubiak to help teach them to quarterback John Elway. But he introduced a different run offense from Bill Walsh's traditional West Coast playbook. Shanahan cast his fortunes with the blocking scheme that had begun taking over the NFL and, to do it, made his most important hire. He hired offensive line coach Alex Gibbs to install a zone-blocking running game.

When Shanahan brought him on to his staff, Gibbs already had the reputation of a guru. He had spent fifteen years coaching college football before another ten or so in the NFL, including a brief stint with Shanahan at the Los Angeles Raiders. What they accomplished in Denver, however, became the stuff of legend: two Super Bowls, several incredible rushing seasons by the out-of-nowhere Terrell Davis, and then many more years when it seemed like the Broncos could take a guy off the street and turn him into a thousand-yard rusher.

After something of a falling-out with Shanahan in 2003, Gibbs took over as the offensive line and running game coach for the Michael Vick–led Atlanta Falcons, where he was similarly successful. During Gibbs's three seasons in Atlanta, the Falcons led the NFL in rushing with more than 8,100 yards. Most impressively, the Falcons were the only team over that three-year period to average more than five yards per rushing attempt.

In his first two seasons in Houston, Kubiak's Texans went 14–18. For his third year, Kubiak brought on Gibbs to orchestrate the running game. Gibbs is gone now—he left Houston after a couple of seasons, then briefly joined Pete Carroll's staff in Seattle before retiring—but the Texans still use the Gibbs formula, which has been good enough to give them the second-best rushing attack in the league this season. What was Gibbs's magic and how can the Texans use it to make a playoff run, even with the NFL equivalent of John Q. Public at quarterback?

The key to Gibbs's zone running game is that the foundational play is the outside zone (the "wide zone," in Gibbs's terminology), not the more common inside zone. The inside zone is a vertical push play that aims to move the defense backward and have a running back carry the ball forward with a full head of steam to get yards. The outside zone is more about lateral movement. Each blocker first steps to the side rather than forward (and many coaches teach their linemen to take their first step backward, a technique referred to as "losing ground to gain ground"). The blockers then try to pin defenders to the inside—or if they can't do that, drive them to the sideline. Sometimes on these plays, the running back runs around the edge on a traditional-looking sweep. More often, the defense is stretched to its limit and the runner hits a crease and then sprints straight toward the end zone. When executed correctly, it's extremely taxing on the defense, as all of their instincts—aggressiveness to the ball carrier and fast pursuit— work against them, and linemen without great size or talent can open huge holes through excellent technique and discipline.

But if it's so good, why doesn't every NFL team use it? The answer is the same reason that, despite his legendary status, Gibbs has never lasted too long in one job. Gibbs's style of zone blocking requires total commitment by every offensive player—linemen must be perfect technicians, not just fat guys who push others around; runners must make reads and make one-cut-and-go rather than juke and tap dance like the next Barry Sanders; and quarterbacks and receivers can't treat runs as breaks because they're expected to execute assignments and make blocks. The offense is also taxing on coaches. Gibbs will tell anyone willing to listen that if you want to be good at the wide zone and the tight zone, throw out all of your other run plays. All those wonderful Power-O plays, counter trey plays, and whatever other fancy stuff you think you need—get rid of it. Instead, run two—yes, two—run plays, and run them against every defensive front you face until you get really good at them. To Gibbs, anything else is hubris.

The Texans run a few other run plays, but the wide zone remains the foundation of their offense. Those big Arian Foster and Ben Tate runs that have powered Houston to the playoffs came on the same plays that helped Davis rush 2,008 yards for the Broncos in 1998 and helped Warrick Dunn, Gibbs's diminutive running back in Atlanta, thrive. So why is it so successful?

Like Gibbs, one can spend a lifetime on the finer details of the outside zone, but we can cover the highlights. On the play, each offensive lineman asks himself: Am I covered? Is there a defender lined up directly across from me? Or am I uncovered? If he's covered, there's really not much zone to it at all. The lineman fires out and blocks the guy in front of him. If he's uncovered, he steps to the play side to help his covered teammate; together, they double-team a defensive lineman until one of them slides off to block a second-level defender like a linebacker.

Those assignments apply to both the inside zone and wide zone. The differences concern technique. On the wide zone, blockers try to reach the defenders and seal them to the inside. If they can't be reached because the defender angles out to the sideline, then the blocker's task is to push the defenders as far as possible toward the sideline, to run him out of the play. On the backside, Gibbs likes to "cut" defenders to the ground—this is sometimes controversial, but it remains legal and is an important key to sealing off the backside pursuit.

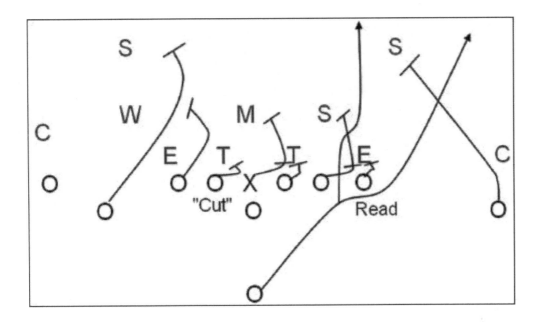

The key then becomes the running back and whether he can find those fluid zones that might open up anywhere across the defensive front. Running backs are often under coached, however, even at the NFL level. On the wide zone, the running back isn't simply handed the ball and told, "Run like hell." He needs to make reads. He looks, in sequence, to the defensive end and then the defensive tackle. His job is to make one cut and get yards depending on their movements. If they stay inside, he runs outside; if they fly outside, he'll cut back, although on the wide zone what looks like a cutback is typically not a cutback at all. Instead, the runner goes straight up the field against a fast-pursuing defense.

This is often a point of contention: NFL running backs reach their position by being the best player on the field their entire lives. As kids and high school stars and often college stars, too, they really were given the ball and told to run like hell. But in the NFL, if they miss their reads on a wide zone, the offense won't work. The running creases may be there, but it won't matter if the runner isn't hitting them properly.

In Denver, Gibbs came up with an elegant solution to this problem. On most teams, each position is coached by direct position coaches. So on the wide zone, the running back was coached only by the running backs coach, and if a player made the wrong read, his teammates didn't necessarily know it. Instead, Gibbs taught the play to the entire team, so that even the offensive linemen knew the running back's reads. This way, if the runner made a bad read, the coach didn't need to step in, because as soon as a play ended the linemen would turn around and yell at the running back. On football teams, as in most places, your peers are often more persuasive—or easier to listen to—than authority figures.

And that's really about it: it's a simple play. It gets more complicated as defenses get more varied and complex. But even after Gibbs, Kubiak remains committed to the wide zone, and Foster and Tate are adept at making the correct reads and hitting the holes at full speed. And all that good running sets up something else— once the defense has overcommitted to the run, there are lots of opportunities for effective bootlegs and play-action schemes, stuff that Schaub did very well. To win some playoff games, Yates, Delhomme, or whoever starts for Houston will have to take advantage of those opportunities.

When Kubiak earned his two Super Bowls with the Denver Broncos, it was an aging but still wily John Elway who served as the counterpunch to the Broncos' base rushing attack. Teams that win Super Bowls typically have great quarterback play, and that's not something the Texans possess now that Schaub is injured. But, fortunately for Yates and Kubiak, there is a little history on their side: in 1990, and with just four prior NFL starts to his name, Jeff Hostetler filled in for an injured Phil Simms and led the New York Giants to a win in Super Bowl XXV. It's a long shot, but if the Texans can make a run, there's a good chance it'll be because of the wide zone and all the opportunities it provides. And with all the attention this season on quarterbacks such as Aaron Rodgers, Tom Brady, and Drew Brees, it'd be nice to see a team like the Texans make a run and claim some of the spotlight for the offensive line.

HOW REX RYAN CREATED THE NEW LOOK
NEW ENGLAND PATRIOTS OFFENSE

FALL 2011

Bill Belichick and his New England Patriots crushed Rex Ryan and his Jets recently, quieting talk of both the impending doom of the Patriots and the surge of the Jets. In watching the game, I was struck by two things. First, that the Patriots managed to destroy the Jets despite being rather awful in several phases of the game—they can't run the ball, and the defense, while it made some plays, is clearly a bizarre assortment of castaways and free agents (at one point late in the game, backup receiver Julian Edelman lined up as a defensive back aligned over a slot receiver). My first thought is whether a team with such obvious flaws can ultimately take home a Super Bowl. But the second thing that jumped out to me is how, by adding tight ends Rob Gronkowski and Aaron Hernandez, Belichick has completely reshaped the style and personality of New England's offense.

Elite NFL teams tend to build around the virtues of their most problematic opponents, and since Rex Ryan took over the Jets and designed his defense around taking target practice at Patriots quarterback Tom Brady, Belichick has had his eye on the Jets. Going into the 2009 season, the Patriots—with Randy Moss on the outside, Wes Welker on the inside, and the near-undefeated season fresh in their minds—had essentially become a pass-first spread offense team in the style of some of the more prominent college teams. Brady made checks at the line and lined up primarily in shotgun, and the offense relied on quick passes and hot reads to defeat blitzes, with Moss the ever-present threat to burn the defense deep. Since they typically lined up with three receivers and only one running back, Ryan was able to specifically attack Brady's pass protection and take away the run along the way. He forced Belichick's hand in terms of play calling: New England's spread to pass became predictable instead of fearsome, and it was up to Brady on almost every play to throw the ball before some unblocked rusher took him down again. So Belichick went out and drafted both Gronkowski and Hernandez.

Hernandez is more of a pure receiver, and his chief advantage is as a substitution/personnel problem: if he's in the game, you don't know if he'll line up as a tight end or if he'll split wide so that Welker can play the slot, forcing you to decide whether to put your cornerback on Welker or Hernandez, potentially creating advantages in both the running and passing games. But Gronkowski is a true triple threat from the tight-end spot: He can block, he can go out for passes, and he can even block and then go out for delayed passes. Multiple defenders therefore have to keep their eyes on him. And against such a threat, Ryan can't sell out with multifarious blitzes overloaded to one side or the other, simply in an all-out effort to get Tom Brady. The presence of the tight ends—where will they line up, what will they do?—dictates terms back to Rex Ryan, who would much rather cut loose and go on carrying his father's torch as the destroyer of pretty-boy quarterbacks.

And this is just one example of what has become a necessity for NFL offenses as defenses have gotten, well, weirder; you must have players who can dictate terms back to the defense by presenting odd matchup problems. The most obvious examples are the hybrid receiver/tight ends like Gronkowski and Hernandez, but also the

Saints' Jimmy Graham, the Packers' Jermichael Finley, and, yes, still, the apparently immortal Tony Gonzalez of the Falcons. (Indeed, Belichick has talked about the difficulties Gonzalez presented in putting together a defensive game plan to defend any team he was on, and Gonzalez may have even inspired the coach to focus more closely on tight ends.) Dynamic runner/receivers like Darren Sproles also create issues for defenses.

Unpredictability is the key. Is a play a run or a pass? Which direction is it going? How will it work? These hybrid weapons give offenses options in ways that even great players with more specific skills and roles cannot. They simplify defenses by making them uncertain. Of course, the problem for NFL teams—and for college or high school teams that want to run a pro-style offense—is finding players who can do all these things. So it's one thing to say they are the future and another to actually find enough people to make that future a reality. Just like the quarterback position, there are simply more job openings than there are qualified candidates. Wanted: six-foot-six freak athlete who can run a 4.5 forty, has incredible hands, is willing and able to block three-hundred-pound defensive ends, and can immediately memorize a thousand-page playbook. No appointment necessary.

PART II

HISTORY

History must be a part of the study… It is a part of the rational study, because it is the first step toward an enlightened scepticism, that is, towards a deliberate reconsideration of the worth of those rules.
When you get the dragon out of his cave on to the plain and in the daylight, you can count his teeth and claws, and see just what is his strength. But to get him out is only the first step. The next is either to kill him, or to tame him and make him a useful animal.

—Oliver Wendell Holmes Jr.

FRANK BEAMER AND BUD FOSTER'S VIRGINIA TECH DEFENSE

FALL 2009

In many ways the spread offense, both in its run-first and pass-first incarnations, was invented to counter the aggressive, eight-man front defense like the one Virginia Tech made famous in the 1990s. Back then, many teams tried to emulate Frank Beamer and defensive coordinator Bud Foster's scheme, with its premium on defenders stacking the line to either stop the run or scare the offense into abandoning it and apologizing for having considered such a silly idea. Yet the spread offense has effectively run the true eight-man front out of college football—at least as a base defense—with its reliance on quick, easy throws along with quarterback runs and its overall "speed in space" philosophy.

But here's the rub: while the defense Virginia Tech made en vogue was effectively countered, the actual schemes Beamer and Foster have put into practice in Blacksburg have evolved, year in and year out, to maintain one of the most dominant defensive legacies in the country. Since joining the Atlantic Coast Conference in 2004, the Hokie D has rebounded from subpar years in 2002 and 2003 to finish in the top ten nationally in both yards and points allowed five years in a row—despite overhauling their base defensive scheme, to zero fanfare. To understand what the Hokies do now, it helps to first understand what they used to do.

Tech was long known as an exemplar of the eight-man front. While many commentators talk about such fronts in terms of simple arithmetic, for Virginia Tech, it was both a scheme and a philosophy. They called their particular scheme, which was first refined at the University of Washington under its former defensive coordinator and head coach Jim Lambright, the "G," and it was a variant of a 4–4 front. This meant that there were four defensive linemen, four linebackers (two inside linebackers and two outside linebackers, still colorfully referred to as the "Whip" and the "Rover"), and three secondary players: two corners and a free safety. "G" referred to the specific alignments of the defensive line and linebackers.

From this eight-at-the-line set, Tech used all manner of blitzes and devices to get defenders into the offense's backfield. They also used all the common pass coverages, like Cover 1 and Cover 3 (the number usually refers to the number of deep zone players—i.e., Cover 3 is literally a three-deep coverage). But Beamer and Foster also relied on a hybrid coverage of their own design: the Robber, run out of the G front. This coverage worked well because it transformed an already run-heavy eight-man front into a nine-man front, where they combined their 4–4 set with conventional two-deep principles: instead of two deep safeties, they used two deep *cornerbacks* who split the field into halves. The free safety then was free to play a Robber technique—that is, on pass plays, he read the quarterback's eyes and broke on intermediate routes, but on runs, where he truly became valuable, he was an incredible *ninth run stuffer* in the box.

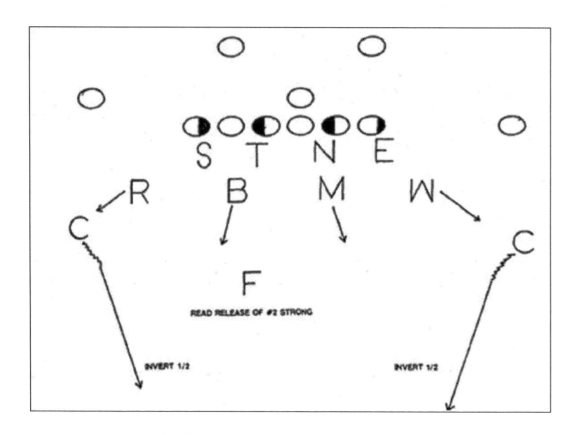

READ RELEASE OF #2 STRONG

INVERT 1/2

INVERT 1/2

Although this defense was not the best against the pass, that wasn't the point. It was good enough (especially with dynamos like D'Angelo Hall at cornerback), and the focus was on stuffing the run or hitting the quarterback before he could release the ball. Unsurprisingly, against such stacked fronts, teams didn't have a prayer of running against the Hokies, and every play seemed like an avalanche of defenders. Also unsurprisingly, however, offensive schemes began to change.

The narrative over the last decade in college ball has been the rise of the spread offense, and, good as it is, the 4–4 Robber G was not designed for the spread offense. With only three secondary players, the defense was limited in what coverages it could use and disguise. As Bud Foster told ESPN's Mark Schlabach, "Back when they played two tailbacks, you could put eight or nine guys in the box. Now they're making it tougher to do that because of where they place their people." And so, he explained, with offenses "putting five or six athletes out in space," the Hokies too had to "put athletes out in space."

He and Beamer did so by converting his Rover outside linebacker, already a hybrid player who sometimes looked more like a strong safety, into a full-time defensive back. This allowed them also to make a dramatic switch away from the coverages they had used—i.e., man-to-man with a deep free safety, or two deep with the corners—to basing from a Cover 4, also known as "quarters" coverage.

As with other coverages, the "4" in Cover 4 refers to the number of defenders dropping into deep zones—in this case, four guys, both corners and both safeties. But don't confuse this with prevent coverage: it's a whirl of contradictions—a zone defense with man-to-man principles, and a defense with four secondary players that can still present a nine-man front against the run.

Quarters can be a four-across deep zone, it can double-team a dangerous wide receiver, or it can be straight man-to-man. What the defense actually employs will be determined by what the offense does. This type of read-and-react is great against the spread's multiplicity, as it can allow some very short completions but lead to lots of interceptions and it permits very few downfield passing windows.

But what of stopping the run? The advantage of the old 4–4 Robber G was as a run-stuffing defense with a nine-man front, and don't many spread teams spread to run the football? What makes Tech's quarters coverage particularly interesting is that they have not actually changed their old G front, they have merely removed one guy from the box and lined him up at safety without changing his aggressive responsibilities against the run. Against a spread-to-run look, the Hokies will line up in their base quarters look from the G, merely moving the former Rover to safety while moving the Whip outside, over the slot receiver, thus giving the offense very little information. And, once the defender reads run, all of those players attack the ballcarrier—fast.

The upshot is that the Hokies' safeties play extremely aggressively against the run from Cover 4—each safety has specific run-game responsibilities and provides run support to both the frontside and backside. Indeed, just the threat of aggression leads to problems for the offense and opens things up for the rest of the defense.

The moral is that Beamer and Foster have continued to stay a step ahead of offenses, and have done so by keeping their eyes wide open and knowing when changes in the way offenses played was imminent. As Foster also told ESPN of the spread, "I think it's here to stay…I don't think it's a fad. It's just part of the evolution of offense." But neither is the Hokies defense a fad, nor a fluke that just stacked the box when everyone was running the ball out of two backs. Defense is just old principles applied to new situations, and so it is with Virginia Tech, where, through disguises, a new base look, and some ideas from their old defenses, the Hokies year in and year out dominate with what's known as the "Lunch Pail Defense." The schemes might change, but the mentality—and the results—haven't.

DICK LEBEAU, DOM CAPERS, AND THE
EVOLUTION OF DEFENSE

SPRING 2011

While the media storyline for Super Bowl 45 (don't even ask about the Roman numeral) is Aaron Rogers versus Ben Roethlisberger, or even Green Bay Packers head coach Mike McCarthy versus Pittsburgh Steelers head coach Mike Tomlin, the cognoscenti understand that the most interesting pairing involves the defensive coordinators, Steelers defensive guru Dick LeBeau and his former protégé and later boss, Dom Capers. Capers, as defensive coordinator for the Steelers, coached with LeBeau back in the early 1990s, where the two men conspired to implement the madcap 3–4 zone blitz schemes that would help LeBeau land in the NFL Hall of Fame. (LeBeau, too, is not without his Green Bay connections, as he was an assistant for the Packers in the late '70s under Bart Starr.) LeBeau took over as Pittsburgh defensive coordinator in 1995 once Capers left to become head coach of the Carolina Panthers.

As is true today, change on defense was spurred on by change on offense. As Tim Layden described in his book *Blood, Sweat & Chalk*, by 1983, the zone blitz didn't take root in the NFL in earnest until after San Francisco 49ers head coach Bill Walsh already had won his first Super Bowl; indeed, he had even won it against

Cincinnati, where LeBeau had been an assistant under Forrest Gregg and later Sam Wyche. While at Cincinnati and faced with precision passing offenses like Walsh's, LeBeau knew his defenses needed to evolve. Before the 1980s, the general but imperfect rule for defenses against passing teams was that a four-man rush meant zone, while a blitz meant man-to-man.

So LeBeau began experimenting with schemes that showed blitz looks—and did in fact rush defenders from unexpected places—but nevertheless dropped a minimum of six defenders into zone coverage. To LeBeau, this was the perfect remedy: depending on the coverage you put behind the blitz, you actually were playing a very conservative defense, but the offense thought you were being aggressive, and, depending on how intelligently you deployed your five rushers, you *were* being aggressive, albeit in a very controlled sense. Controlled chaos, indeed.

But these were still merely dabblings. The next evolution came via a visit to Baton Rouge and Louisiana State University, where former Don Shula assistant and walking repository of football knowledge Bill Arnsparger coached. Arnsparger had experimented with zone blitz schemes for much of the prior fifteen years, including during the Miami Dolphins' undefeated season. According to Layden and LeBeau, Arnsparger kept using the term "safe pressure" to describe the zone blitz, words that stuck with LeBeau: in short, the idea behind the zone blitz was that it *wasn't* a kamikaze defense, but instead merely sound—and conservative—football mixed with disruption. LeBeau would go on to develop these ideas for the next couple of decades, aided by an assistant in Pittsburgh named Dom Capers; LeBeau is the biggest reason, in my view, that Pittsburgh is headed to its third Super Bowl in six years.

With this background, it's worth spending a bit more time on what the zone blitz is and how LeBeau and Capers use it. The basic concept is not new at all: confusing the offense with respect to which defenders are dropping and which are blitzing goes back at least fifty years, and safe coverage in and of itself is an idea just as old, if not another fifty years older. But under a modern understanding, the basic "fire zone blitz" combines (relatively) soft, passive coverage with three deep defenders. This is how the defense, despite being labeled a blitz and thought of as very aggressive, is actually quite conservative—the offense should not be able to get big pass plays down the field. This is not a gambling, go-for-broke scheme in which you dare the other team to make a big play. Note too that one of the advantages of zone blitzing from a 3–4 front (three defensive linemen, four linebackers) is that you do not need to drop a defensive lineman who might not be very good at pass coverage; teams that run a 4–3 (four defensive linemen, three linebackers) generally must.

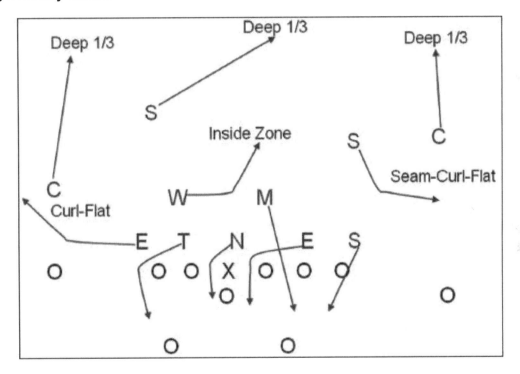

Teams like the Steelers and Green Bay are confident that they can both play zone and also get pressure with only five rushers because they will use those five rushers intelligently. This is where fire zones become multifarious and also where the action is with respect to confusing quarterbacks. Although the basic framework of rushing five guys and dropping six almost never changes, the best defensive coordinators surgically diagnose the other team's protection schemes and design ways for their five attacking defenders to confuse and break free an extra rusher against six or even seven pass protectors—what should be an advantage for the offense.

Regarding coverage, the secondary makes a simple invert rotation, meaning that one safety rotates down to be an intermediate defender. He is joined by two more underneath pass defenders. While each is responsible for a zone, each will also play something of a man-to-man technique on any receiver who enters their zone. Much of the preparation for a game will have been spent on the specific pass-game concepts the defense expects to face so that the defense will defend pass plays themselves rather than simply attempt to follow receivers around. Note too that the defense can use different combinations of defenders in coverage: the five rushers might consist of linemen, linebackers, or defensive backs—it's all a matter of filling the blanks in terms of who is deep, who is intermediate, and who is rushing the quarterback.

When defensive coordinators call blitzes, they do not solely tell the pass rushers to get to the quarterback. Instead, they designate the gap the defender is to attack. This is so they can coordinate the blitz as a whole—so they can attack schematic weaknesses they see in the offense—and also coordinate the blitz in a way that accounts for all the gaps, or holes between linemen, in case the offense runs the ball.

Lastly, a major key to making the zone blitz work is that any defender who is expected to rush but does not—such as a defensive lineman—must step up first before retreating to the zone: the point is to occupy or consume a potential pass blocker by making him hesitate while some other player rushes from elsewhere. If done correctly, an offensive lineman might end up blocking no one at all while some blitzer flies in unblocked. This is why the zone blitz, despite being thought of as safe pressure, so often looks like Ragnarok to the offense and opposing quarterback.

This weekend's Super Bowl will likely turn on how well the quarterbacks (and offensive lines) handle these pressures. Both Capers and LeBeau are old hats and no doubt have spent the last two weeks doodling up great stuff. Then again, the offensive staffs for Pittsburgh and Green Bay have the ultimate resources when it comes to preparing for LeBeau and Capers: the advice and counsel of the other's soul (or blitz) mates. How that will play out is anyone's guess. Regardless of the game's outcome, however, the zone blitz is here to stay. Happy blitzing.

HOW ED REED AND TROY POLAMALU CHANGED THE SAFETY POSITION... AND CHANGED DEFENSES

FALL 2011

Ed Reed and Troy Polamalu seem to have supernatural powers—they're everywhere on the football field at once, omnipresent demigods determined to knock your chinstrap off. Their range of skills is remarkable: total tackles, interceptions (Reed led the NFL in picks in 2010 despite playing only ten games), and even sacks (Polamalu owns the record for most sacks by a safety in an NFL game with three). They play slightly different positions—Reed is a free safety and Polamalu is a strong safety—but that distinction means little to opposing quarterbacks. To them, Reed and Polamalu are men of mayhem, hungry for prey. Their success is a credit to their talent and work ethic, but is also the result of defensive strategies that have helped them make their marks.

Football defenses have been reacting to offenses for more than a century, and there is very little in today's game that wasn't around fifty years ago. Indeed, almost all modern NFL defenses are indebted to the 4–3 defense—referring to four defensive linemen and three linebackers—that Hall of Fame coach Tom Landry invented while serving as defensive coordinator for the New York Giants in the 1950s. This pro-style 4–3 defense continues to evolve —along with its cousin, the 3–4—but Landry's basic scheme of a dynamic seven-man front supported by four flexible secondary players remains to this day.

For the sake of brevity, allow me to oversimplify some history and jump forward a few decades from the inception of Landry's 4–3: By the mid-1980s, offenses had gained an upper hand. Defenses struggled to simultaneously deal with power football—that of fullbacks, tight ends, and pulling linemen—that were coupled with increasingly efficient passing offenses like the one designed by the San Francisco 49ers' Bill Walsh. The best-known (and, for a time, the most effective) response to these developments was the "46" defense implemented by Chicago Bears defensive coordinator Buddy Ryan. The theory behind the 46 was that offenses seized the advantage because defenses let them dictate terms. For thirty years, defenses more or less tried to match and mirror offenses based on personnel and alignment, but they couldn't keep up. Ryan planned to negate this advantage by force—the 46's simple guiding principle was to kick ass.

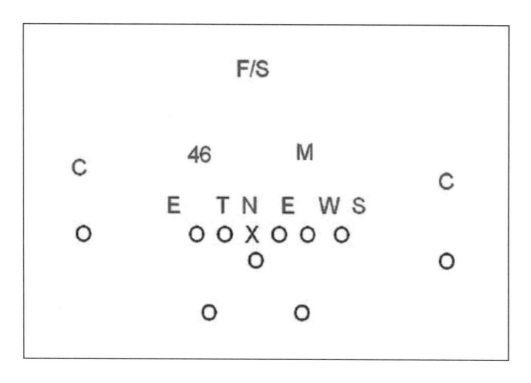

The 1985 Bears, using Ryan's 46 in increasing doses throughout the season, fielded what may have been the greatest defense in NFL history en route to a Super Bowl victory. Yet the name "46," unlike the 4–3 or 3–4, didn't refer to the defensive alignment. Instead, it referred to the guy who wore jersey #46, Doug Plank, Chicago's clever and feisty strong safety. In the 46, Plank was moved out of the pure secondary and became a kind of linebacker. This allowed the Bears defense to put more defenders on the line of scrimmage than the offense could block on both runs and passes. Instead of matching the offense, the 46 sought to overwhelm it. And that season, the Bears did just that.

But, as they always do, offenses adapted to the 46. Spread formations and quick passes became serious challenges for defenses. Even Buddy Ryan, who became head coach of the Philadelphia Eagles in 1986, found his beloved 46 defused by spread concepts and had to cease using it as an every-down defense. By the 1990s, defenses could no longer afford to predictably line up in eight-man fronts like the 46. In response, teams—most notably Tony Dungy's Tampa Bay Buccaneers—developed an approach that took away the short throws to the flats and deep passes that had given the eight-man front so many problems. They did this by using a two-deep coverage look while sending the middle linebacker deep down the center of the field to take away passes to the tight end. Thus, football pundits—particularly of the television variety—had a new catchphrase: the Tampa Two. In this defense, safeties played deep to stop the big play.

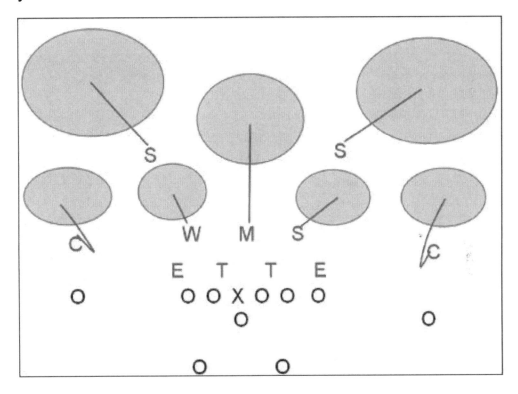

The Tampa Two, however, with two or three deep defenders, was weak against inside runs, and by the early 2000s offenses were too good to let you so obviously declare your intention. Even defenses that switched between eight-man fronts and two-deep coverages had trouble, since offenses could read the defense and shift between spread schemes and power formations. Defenses needed something better. They needed Ed Reed and Troy Polamalu.

Reed and Polamalu were part of a new breed of safety that could do everything a defensive coordinator needed. They could be Doug Plank in the 46 on one play and a deep Tampa Two defender on the next. Defenses knew how to play pass coverage, but they couldn't figure out how to do it while also holding strong against the run. The answer—made possible by these game-changing safeties—came in the form of Cover 4, also known as quarters. It's the most important defensive scheme of the past decade.

At first glance, Cover 4 looks like an anti-pass prevent tactic, with four secondary defenders playing deep. But therein lies its magic. The four defenders are actually playing a matchup zone concept, in which the safety reads the tight end or inside receiver. If an offensive player lined up inside releases on a short pass route or doesn't release into the route, the safety can help double-team the outside receiver. If the inside receiver breaks straight downfield, it becomes more like man coverage. This variance keeps quarterbacks guessing and prevents defenses from being exploited by common pass plays like four verticals, which killed eight-man fronts. The real key to Cover 4, however, is that against the run both safeties become rush defenders (remember, the outside cornerbacks play deep). This allows defenses to play nine men in the box against the run—a hat-tip to the 46's overwhelming force.

This last point is crucial to why Polamalu and Reed thrive in Cover 4. Both safeties have responsibilities against the run; which role they take depends on which way the ball goes. If the running back rushes toward them, they usually have "force" responsibility. If the running back rushes away from them, they're responsible for covering the cutback and bootleg. The interior defenders are typically given "gap" responsibilities to plug the holes they expect to encounter against a specific run play. Those inside defenders typically use something called a spill technique, meaning they chase the running back toward the sideline, where he can be cornered and gang-tackled. But if you're going to force a runner to the outside, you better have someone waiting for him there. That player is the force player, and in Cover 4, it is typically the safety, who has read the run and is in position to crush the ball carrier. Or at the least force him back into the linemen's arms.

The backside safety's job is even more important. He, too, will drop down for the run, but will do so cautiously as he looks to defend against a cutback. Many of the biggest runs in football come not in the initial burst but instead from the runner cutting back in the opposite direction once the defense has over pursued, and it's that backside safety's job to be a sure tackler in space, something Reed and Polamalu do very well. With the safeties in support, the rest of the defenders can swarm the ball carrier. Of course, Cover 4 is but one tactic defensive coordinators can use. Pittsburgh, for example, mixes up its looks by sending Polamalu on a timely zone blitz straight up the middle to either stuff the run or bum-rush the quarterback. Such variety is crucial, but Cover 4 has become one of the most important tactics for modern NFL defenses.

The history of football is essentially the history of ideas meeting talent meeting a moment. Decades of strategic tug-of-war preceded Reed's and Polamalu's careers, and they arrived at a point in the game's development when their skills were particularly needed. Their versatility in defending both pass and run plays allowed NFL defenses to claim victory in one of these strategic battles. Reed and Polamalu have had the good fortune of playing for excellent coaches, but they're also both so talented that they have bent coaches' schemes to their strengths and ruined opponents' carefully designed game plans. This is the beauty of watching these future Hall of Famers play: in every interception, in every tackle for a loss, in every big hit and big return, football history is not only made, but also extended. Their brilliance on the field will continue to inspire the film room schemers to innovate, and football history will continue to be pushed by the twin forces of ideas and athleticism.

VICTOR CRUZ, THE NEW YORK GIANTS, AND THE ADAPTATION (AND ASSIMILATION) OF THE RUN-AND-SHOOT

SPRING 2012

New York Giants wide receiver Victor Cruz has been nothing short of a phenomenon this year. In 2010, his first season, the undrafted free agent had the kind of woulda-coulda-shoulda start to an NFL career that more often leads to telling your grandkids that you almost made it rather than to a fruitful career. Cruz followed a breakout preseason game against the New York Jets—145 receiving yards and three touchdowns—with a season-ending injury. "Your grandfather once played for the Giants! I scored three touchdowns in one game!"

After that, little was expected of the undersized and unheralded receiver who claims to be six-foot-one in cleats. But in 2011 Cruz returned and delivered one of the most remarkable seasons for a receiver in recent memory. He racked up 1,536 yards on eighty-two catches for a staggering 18.7 yards per catch and produced some of the season's most memorable plays, like a ninety-nine-yard touchdown against the Jets and a seventy-four yarder against the

Cowboys in Week 17 that helped propel the Giants into the playoffs. And, of course, he capped off each score with his patented salsa dance, which is the only touchdown move I've seen be analyzed by a dance instructor. It all amounts to a pretty good bedtime story.

Cruz's success is even more fascinating for how he accomplished it. He put up huge numbers by playing what has historically been an unheralded spot—the slot receiver. Cruz lines up inside rather than on the outside of a formation. This season, Cruz's production is not quite as unusual, since several of the league's top receivers played some form of inside receiver spot, whether it was Wes Welker or Rob Gronkowski or Jimmy Graham. Even so, the classic image of a great wide receiver isn't a diminutive speedster lined up in the slot; it's Calvin Johnson or Jerry Rice— bigger, more physical receivers lined up out wide and ready to streak down the sideline or run a deep route. Yet Cruz's success is in no way unprecedented. Indeed, Cruz is the latest in a long line of slot receivers who have operated within the run-and-shoot offense, which forms the backbone of the Giants' passing attack.

The run-and-shoot was supposed to be dead, at least in the NFL. The offense (at least one form of it) was conceived by Glenn "Tiger" Ellison back in the 1950s, while Darrel "Mouse" Davis developed its modern form throughout a four-decade coaching career that has touched nearly every level of football imaginable. The offense had its moment of glory in the NFL in the early 1990s. Back then, the Detroit Lions, Atlanta Falcons, and Houston Oilers (and the Seattle Seahawks, extremely briefly) ran the 'shoot, which featured four wide receivers and one running back on every snap. The offense used no fullbacks and no tight ends. These teams had mixed success. The Lions won twelve games in 1991; the Falcons won ten and made the playoffs twice during their 'shoot days. But the NFL team that most exemplified the run-and-shoot, in both its glory and its shame, was the Houston Oilers. The Oilers made the playoffs in seven straight years with the run-and-shoot (and fielded a top ten offense in each season), and quarterback Warren Moon blitzkrieged defenses with his four-receiver aerial assault. But the Oilers never reached the Super Bowl, and they managed to be on the wrong end of the greatest playoff comeback in NFL history. Against the Buffalo Bills in the 1993 wild-card round, Moon threw four first-half touchdowns, but he wasn't able to burn the clock and the defense collapsed in the second half of a 41–38 loss. The Oilers became part of an even more ignominious moment the following year, when Buddy Ryan, Houston's defensive coordinator, punched the team's offensive coordinator in the face. Ryan was no fan of the run-and-shoot, which he called the "chuck-and-duck."

Eventually, a consensus formed around the league that a team couldn't win championships with the run-and-shoot, and teams abandoned the offense. Without a tight end or fullback, they said, the 'shoot was "finesse only" and lacked the physical element necessary to win. But not everyone agreed. When Hall of Fame safety Rod Woodson heard Houston had given up on the offense, he said: "Tell the owner thank you, and tell the front office thank you. The run-and-shoot got the Oilers where they are, and I think defenses all over the league are going to be very relieved when they hear about it."

But the run-and-shoot went out of fashion for a reason. In a modern NFL full of tight ends and multiple formations, an offense that limits itself to one personnel grouping—whether it's four receivers and one running back or two running backs and a tight end —can't be successful. The run-and-shoot forced the Oilers, Lions, and Falcons to protect their quarterbacks with six players; without multiple looks, today's defenses would develop schemes to destroy those protections. Indeed, what killed the run-and-shoot wasn't the playoff failures or the perceived lack of physicality, but rather the zone blitz, which was designed to defuse the kind of six-man protection schemes that run-and-shoot teams used on every down. For a while, at least, everyone around football seemed to agree that the run-and-shoot had died and would never come back. But the run-and-shoot never left. No, I'm not talking about the increased use of multiple receiver sets or the emphasis on passing in this year's NFL. Both trends exist, but they aren't necessarily tied to the run-and-shoot. Instead, I'm referring to the famous route packages that Mouse Davis invented and every 'shoot team since has used: Streak, Switch, Go, Choice, and so on. What made the 'shoot special—and truly explosive—was that it was backyard football writ to the NFL. Instead of the traditional pro football approach, where a team might have hundreds of pass plays, each with multiple variations, that the quarterbacks and receivers were all required to practice and memorize, the run-and-shoot was simple.

Tiger Ellison's 1950s book on the run-and-shoot described the coach's experience of going to a playground to watch how kids actually play football outside of organized teams. He didn't see anyone getting in a power formation and running the ball off tackle. Instead, he saw the kid with the best arm run around and search for someone to throw the ball to. The receivers had no predetermined routes; they just looked for open areas and ran to get away from their defenders. Ellison had a revelation: high-level football shouldn't have to fight this impulse. It should be based on what comes naturally to every kid who picks up a ball. And thus the run-and-shoot was born.

Prior to Ellison's insight, the great leaps in football strategy had been rooted in increased organization, increased precision, and increased discipline. Coaches like the great Paul Brown of the Cleveland Browns drew on the lessons of World War II—and installed martial-style techniques like huddles, playbooks, game plans, and rigorous drilling. Football, with its brief outbreaks of battle and long stretches of quiet planning, is more steeped in militaristic virtues than any other sport.

Ellison saw another strand running through the game, one closer to rugby, football's Continental forebear, as well as sports like basketball and soccer where fluid, on-the-fly athletic intelligence matters as much as planning. While teams like the Browns achieved victory with the inevitability of a Roman legion marching through some soon-to-be-conquered territory, Ellison's "Now Attack" was ad hoc guerrilla warfare.

Mouse Davis organized Ellison's insights into the offense the Oilers ran forty years later, and he did so by combining Brown's military approach with Ellison's free-flowing game. Each pass play was designed with the rigor of Brown's battle plans, but instead of a single assignment, each wide receiver was given a decision tree. If the play was Go, the slot receiver might run deep; he might stop and turn back to the quarterback after about eight yards; he might run ten or twelve yards and then break across the field; or he might go deep, but instead of going straight he'd run diagonally upfield. Ultimately, the decision didn't really belong to the receiver. Just like backyard football, it depended on the defense. Just as Ellison taught, while a receiver might have a variety of different assignments on a given play, he is ultimately given one overarching, all-encompassing command: get open.

It's true that the pure run-and-shoot is never coming back to the NFL. But this aspect of the offense—the read-and-react style that rang up huge numbers in the early 1990s—has never left. It was merely co-opted into other attacks. For an offense that is supposedly defunct, it may be surprising to know that almost every team in the NFL uses some piece of the old Oilers offense, whether it is a type of read route or an entire concept. In this way, Victor Cruz and the Giants' success is no surprise. Cruz is a current-day version of former Oiler Ernest Givins—the gutsy, undersized slot receiver who has a knack for reading defenses (and uses that skill to shatter receiving records). And let's not forget the name of the Oilers offensive coordinator at whom Buddy Ryan took a swing: it was Kevin Gilbride, offensive coordinator for the 2011–12 New York Giants.

After leaving the Oilers, Gilbride joined the expansion Jacksonville Jaguars under their new head coach, Tom Coughlin. Given the sorry history of expansion franchises, they searched for an offense that would give the Jaguars an edge. Coughlin had no interest in running the "chuck-and-duck," but over the next few seasons, Gilbride and Coughlin blended their styles into an attack that helped Mark Brunell lead the league in passing in the franchise's second season and brought Jacksonville to the AFC championship game twice. Gilbride left after the 1996 season and bounced around as a coordinator before reuniting with Coughlin in New York.

The Giants' offense is different from what Coughlin and Gilbride ran in Jacksonville, but it retains many of the same elements: a mixture of traditional sets and spread looks, along with several old run-and-shoot favorites. As long as Coughlin coaches the Giants, they will be a run-first team, but it's also clear that this season's Eli Manning–led passing attack has been the one constant for an inconsistent 9–7 team that now hopes to complete another run from the wild card to the Super Bowl.

Cruz is the player who makes the New York offense truly dynamic. From his slot receiver position, it's his job to, well, get open. Earlier this season, when Gilbride described Cruz's job and development on the field, it sounded like a flashback to the run-and-shoot Oilers:

> When you are in that inside position and that is where we needed somebody to be, there is a lot going on. It is so much easier outside because you have a corner, and if the corner goes deep or rolls up and the safety is over the top, that is it. But inside you have somebody over your head, you have a linebacker, a safety and the other safety across, you have so many more variables in the equation of [Cruz] making the final decision…[Cruz] has really reduced the number of errors he makes and he is making a lot of good decisions, and you saw the great plays… He is doing the right things and I am really proud of him and what has taken place because I don't know how fair it was to expect so much. We always knew we had a guy that we knew could do it but you never know if they are going to do it.

A perfect example of Cruz excelling in a run-and-shoot play this season came in Week 3 against the Eagles. On third-and-two, Gilbride called an old staple—the Switch concept. At the snap, the inside receiver, Cruz, and the outside receiver, Hakeem Nicks, were to switch their releases by crisscrossing past each other. But that's just where the fun begins. Each receiver still had multiple decisions to make. Nicks's job was to run an inside "seam read" route. Depending on how the defense played him, Nicks might go vertical or he might break across the field. Cruz's first responsibility was to get deep, but if the defense played him over the top to take away the deep ball, his job was to stop and look for a pass in the open space. On the play, the Eagles blitzed and Cruz found an open spot in the defense and waited. Manning found him, and seventy-four yards and several broken tackles later, the Giants had a touchdown.

The following image is an actual page from Coughlin and Gilbride's playbook with the Jaguars, showing how they ran the old switch in modern football with a tight end.

8/9 SLOT WIDE 76/7 SWITCH W DRIVE

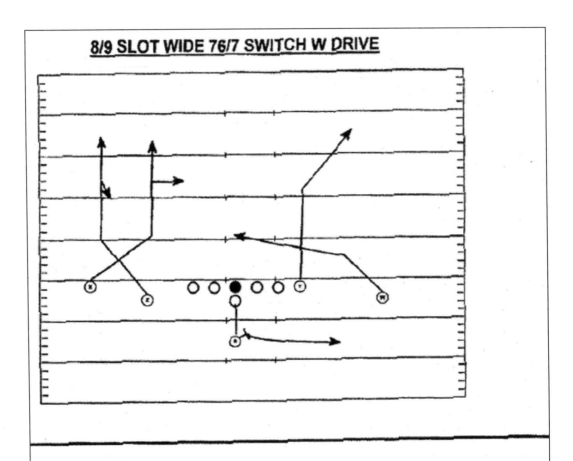

QB: COACHING POINT: 5 Step Drop. Base Progression Read of X-Z-W. Alert Flag to Y Vs. Press on W.

X: Release inside to seam Area. Execute Inside Streak Read.

Z: Release under X, Push vertical reading coverage to either Hook Up, or Take it through.

Y: Execute 12 yard Flag Route.

W: Execute Drive Route.

R: Block Protection - N/T Execute Swing Route.

Examples of these run-and-shoot concepts abound in the Giants' game plans. Cruz reads the defense on almost every pass play, and the Giants' favorite formation to pass from incorporates a variation on the run-and-shoot's Choice concept, with Hakeem Nicks as a single backside receiver with multiple route options while three receivers to the other side run a different combination of pass routes. This forces defenses to pick their poison: guard Nicks one-on-one and Manning will throw to him all day, just as Warren Moon once did with guys like Haywood Jeffires. If the defense sends additional players to Nicks's side, space opens up for the run game inside or for the other receivers, just as it did for Cruz on his ninety-nine-yard touchdown against the Jets. For a dead offense, that's pretty good.

In football, the narrative is never as simple as it seems. Do the Giants run the run-and-shoot? No, of course not. But they use pieces of it, just as every other NFL team does. Drew Brees's best pass play is four verticals, where the receivers can adjust on the fly —a 'shoot staple; the Patriots use a plethora of option routes, where receivers are given the freedom to get open and break in any direction they want; and even Peyton Manning's great Colts offenses frequently asked receivers to read routes on the fly. Maybe these players and coaches use run-and-shoot concepts without knowing where they came from, but they use them.

There are few absolute truths in football. One is that championships are won with talent and hard work more than anything else. Another is that good ideas don't die. They merely get assimilated. This year's Giants are the proof.

PART III

THEORY

In theory there is no difference between theory and practice. In practice there is.

—Yogi Berra

THE CONSTRAINT THEORY
OF OFFENSE

———

SUMMER 2011

———

What kind of offense should you (or do you) run? A typical response sounds something like the following: "I run a system with bubble screens, play action passes, screens, and draws." This is a nonsensical answer. That's not an offense; it's a collection of plays. An offense consists of what are your base runs, base drop back passes, base options, or other base, core plays. The other plays I mentioned are not your offense, they are constraints on the defense, or "constraint plays".

The idea is that you have certain plays that always work on the whiteboard against the defense you hope to see—the pass play that always works against Cover 3, the run play that works against the 4–3 under without the linebackers cheating inside. Yes, it is what works on paper. But we don't live in a perfect world: the constraint plays are designed to make sure you live in one that is as close as possible to the world you want, the world on the whiteboard.

Constraint plays thus work on defenders who cheat. For example, the safety might get tired of watching you break big runs up the middle, so he begins to cheat up. Now you call play action and make him pay for his impatience. The outside linebackers cheat in for the same reason: to stop the run. Now you throw the bubble screen, run the bootleg passes to the flat, and make them pay for their impatience. Now the defensive ends begin rushing hard upfield; you trap, draw, and screen them to make them pay for getting out of position. If that defensive end played honest, your tackle could block him; if he flies upfield, your tackle cannot. Constraint plays make them get back to basics. Once they get back to playing honest football, you go back to the whiteboard and beat them with your bread and butter.

In a given game, your offense might look like it is all constraint plays: all gimmicks, screens, traps, draws, fakes, and the like. Maybe so, if that's what the defense deserves. But you can't lose sight of the structure of your offense. Just because the bubbles, the flares, the fakes, and the other gimmicks are your best offense for a couple of weeks doesn't mean that they will work against a defense that plays soundly. The best defense against that kind of stuff is a simple, disciplined one. Great offenses therefore must be structured around sound, time-tested core ideas, but with the added flexibility to go to the constraint plays whenever the opportunity exists. Unfortunately, even at football's highest levels, the constraint plays are alternatively given too much and not enough weight. But they nevertheless are what make an offense go.

If you're a drop back pass team—think of the Air Raid guys like Mike Leach—you need constraint plays to counteract defenses that cheat for the passes. If you're a great run team, you need constraints to attack safeties and linebackers who all cheat by formation and post-snap effort to stop your run game. You must have the counters, the screens, the bootlegs, and the quick passes. These constraint plays are most important against the best defenses because those teams put the biggest premium on taking away what you hang your hat on. (But be wary of constraint plays against very talented teams—they may be stuffing your core offense not because they are cheating, but instead because they are better than you; the constraint plays then play into their hands.)

The upshot is that a good offense must: (1) find those one or two things on which it will hang its hat on to beat any "honest" defense—think of core pass plays, options, and so on, while it also (2) must get good at all those little constraint plays that keep the defense honest. You won't win any championships simply throwing the bubble screen, but the bubble will help keep you from losing games when the defense wants to crush your run game. Same goes for draws and screens if you're a passing team. You find ways to do what you want and put your players in position to win and score.

Designing an offense is all about structure. Constraint plays, like the bubble, work when the defense gives you the play by how it is lined up; same for play-action passes over the top. When I say these are defensive cheats, I mean they aren't the base, whiteboard defenses you expect because defenses—both players and coaches —adjust to take away what you do well. But you want to go to your core stuff, so you build your offense off of that, and each constraint play forces the defense back in line, right where you want them. That's the beauty of football: punch, counterpunch.

FOOTBALL AND DECISION MAKING

SUMMER 2009

One of the many reasons that football is the greatest of all games is that it encompasses every type of decision humans are capable of. There are the carefully planned decisions coaches make leading up to a game: Who should start? What will our opening plays look like? How can we defend against this scheme? There are the snap, in-the-moment athletic judgments: Who has the ball? Is the receiver open? Is the hole inside the guard or outside it? Where will the running crease be? And there are what I call "golf swing decisions," which combine a reflective moment with a snap athletic judgment: When should I snap the ball to time up with the motion man, while still getting off a good snap? I need to blitz through the A gap between guard and center, but what if they are in a slide or gap protection scheme and close that off? Should I try a rip- or swim-type move? I'm a receiver and need to run an out route, but if the cornerback comes up and jams me and I need to run a go route, how should I use my hands, eyes, etc.?

Football shares the need for snap athletic judgments with most other sports, like basketball or soccer. But it is unique in that every four- to six-second contest is bracketed by a complete stoppage of play where everyone has some time to collect their thoughts—or to

70

heighten their anxieties. Baseball has some of this, insofar as pitchers have to think about the type of pitch they want to throw, but even if batters could get a handle on the pitchers' rhythm, the human brain cannot rationally break down the throw is when it is coming in at ninety miles per hour—it must be an instinctual swing-or-don't response.

Very rarely does a football player use his rational brain during a play in the way he would in solving a math problem. Jonah Lehrer, in his book *How We Decide*, tells a story about Tom Brady. He describes Brady's mind-set as an elite quarterback in the pocket as —especially considering that quarterback is considered maybe the most intellectually demanding of all sports positions—surprisingly instinctual and unthinking. Brady drops back and scans his receivers. He gets to one and simply lets the ball go. Brady is asked: "Why did you throw it to that guy?" He replies: "I just felt like he was open." That's it? That's it.

There really can't be much more to it than that. A quarterback might have an idea of where he might throw it, as his rational brain can do some early legwork, but the ultimate decision—during a play —is by the emotional, reactive parts of his brain. The brain, getting some kind of positive feedback, tells the muscles to release the ball. And how could it be otherwise? These decisions happen much too fast for any person to coldly and rationally walk their way through it. The quarterback must simply know.

This need for amazing decision making that is nevertheless largely reactive is one reason why it is so difficult to evaluate quarterbacks—or any player. You only get so far by asking Tom Brady "Why did you throw it to him?" when his answer is "I felt like he was open." And that's with quarterbacks, the players who are expected in popular culture to be the brains of the team or the "coaches on the field." If that is true of them, obviously safeties on defense, linebackers, linemen, running backs, and receivers all rely more on this same raw, emotional intelligence than they do on something coldly rational. How do you measure that kind of

71

instinctive, nondescriptive intelligence? What is particularly scary is that if a guy does not possess this kind of nonrational ability to make such decisions, he will kill your team with bad "decisions," and coaches get fired for not teaching the quarterback how to do something that is unexplainable in words.

Yet what does the NFL use to evaluate its players' intelligences? The Wonderlic Test. In a world where not even Tom Brady's athletic intelligence is necessarily rational or describable in the way a mathematician's or philosopher's is, how useful can this test be? Yes, it can help eliminate some total knuckleheads, in that NFL players must learn large playbooks (and in college must be able to stay eligible lest the idea of student-athlete be completely severed), but most of what makes them elite or not is based on how they react, not on how they take written tests.

When a linebacker just knows that a play-action fake is indeed a fake, or that the running back still has the ball after misdirection from a wide receiver faking a reverse, he uses very little if any of the skills tested by the Wonderlic. Yet I sympathize with the NFL: how else would you test this stuff? But what if having a really high rational intelligence not only didn't help or didn't test what made a player good or great, what if a heightened analytical ability made a player worse?

This is where "golf swing" intelligence comes in, known casually as "paralysis by analysis." Think about getting ready to swing a golf club while a friend or pro tries to coach you on an innumerable number of tiny physical points that you must somehow keep in your mind—your rational brain—all at once, while making your body comply: "Keep your arms straight"; "Turn your hips"; "Keep your head down"; "Keep the club face square"; "Choke down on the club"; "Loosen your grip"; "Bring your arms through before you start moving your shoulders, but keep your head down"; "Keep the club face square but also rotate your wrists so that you finish with a good rotation." I heard a story about one such instruction setting, where the pro offered a would-be golfer a similar list of such considerations to take into account while swinging his club. The golfer just stood there, club in hand, paralyzed. The pro asked, "What are you thinking about?" The reply: "All the stuff you just told me."

What makes all of this even more impenetrable and mysterious are the kinds of questions we ask of athletes after games: "What were you thinking out there?" "What did it feel like?" The answers, of course, are almost always silly: "I just took it one play at a time. Kept doing my best. Focused on the basics, you know." "I'm just really happy. We've all worked really hard." And what use is it to ask a receiver, "What was going through your mind?" after he made a leaping, diving, tumbling catch in a big game, or to ask of a running back, "What were you thinking on that touchdown run?" Frankly, I'd be scared if they said they'd been thinking about some Henry James novel or an article in the *Economist* that they'd read recently, just as much as I would be if they tried to say they focused on the exact rotation speed of the ball and that they needed to calibrate the position of their hands in some particular way or at some angle to catch it. The reality is that something primordial went through the player's brain: "Ball in air, I have a chance, catch it." The actual signals and responses flowing from the brain and to the body and back are amazing and beautiful, but they aren't what one would describe as rational.

This is not to say that this pre-rational basis for most football decisions is bad, it is that it is so hard to evaluate or even to describe. This is of practical import for college and NFL scouts, who end up saying ridiculous things simply because there is often so little to cogently say. Their judgment about a player—that he is not fast enough, that he doesn't make good enough decisions, that he doesn't make enough big plays—may be accurate, but the lengths to which the descriptions go often add very little to the analysis. And even more troubling, the players *themselves* often can't even describe what they've done.

The late David Foster Wallace discussed this in a review of a biography about tennis prodigy Tracy Austin. As Wallace put it, athletic genius might not only be distinct from rational genius, it might even be the antithesis of it:

> It remains very hard for me to reconcile the vapidity of [an athlete's] narrative mind, on the one hand, with the extraordinary mental powers that are required by world-class tennis, on the other. Anyone who buys into the idea that great athletes are dim should have a close look at an NFL playbook, or at a basketball coach's diagram of a 3–2 zone trap…It is not an accident that great athletes are often called "naturals," because they can, in performance, be totally present: they can proceed on instinct and muscle-memory and autonomic will such that agent and action are one…The real secret behind top athletes' genius, then, may be as esoteric and obvious and dull and profound as silence itself. The real, many-veiled answer to the question of just what goes through a great player's mind as he stands at the center of hostile crowd-noise and lines up the free-throw that will decide the game might well be: nothing at all…This is, for me, the real mystery—whether such a person is an idiot or a mystic or both and/or neither…It may be that… those who receive and act out the gift of athletic genius must, perforce, be blind and dumb about it—and not because blindness and dumbness are the price of the gift, but because they are its essence.

We marvel at athletic genius, we try to understand it, to coach it, to replicate it, but it may be that it is all beyond description. I'm reminded of a quote from a friend who is a defensive coordinator in high school. When asked what kind of players he best likes to coach, he told me: "Give me the 2.5 GPA kids. I'll take them all day, everyday. Smart enough to know what's going on, too dumb to know when something is going to hurt, and not smart enough to remember what hurt last time."

WHY SPIKING THE BALL IS ALMOST ALWAYS A BAD IDEA

SPRING 2012

Football announcers have many annoying habits and verbal tics, from overdescription of what is happening on the field to the substitution of clichés for analysis. And, for some reason, almost every announcer loves to tell us, when a team that is trailing its opponent during the waning moments of a game has gotten a positive play, that "now it's time for them to go up there and spike the ball!"—which is, more often than not, precisely the wrong advice. Spiking the ball is such a simple, seemingly straightforward act, but a little thought reveals how crucial and even complex the decision can be. First, when you spike the ball, you have no idea how valuable the down you are losing might be, and, second, although it's true for some teams that spiking the ball might take less time than just lining up and calling a play at the line, there is no reason that that should be the case; in the age of no-huddle offenses, it should not take more time to call a play like "Red 92!" or "81 Dragon!" than it takes to scream out "Spike play! Spike play!"

Indeed, the late Homer Smith, the former offensive coordinator for UCLA and Alabama who has published books on the subject of clock management, frequently made the further but crucial point that *the spike play itself uses time off the clock*. As Coach Smith put it:

"Even when there is not time to use all four downs and even if you can snap the ball for a regular play as fast as you can snap it for the spike, it consumes a second that might have otherwise allowed you an additional play."

Examples of costly spike plays abound every weekend of the season, at nearly every level. Maybe most famously, the 1998 Rose Bowl between Washington State, led by head coach Mike Price and quarterback Ryan Leaf, and Michigan, who would share in the national title that year, ended rather controversially. Washington State, trailing 21–16, was driving in a desperate attempt to take the lead. With eight seconds left, Ryan Leaf tossed a short hitch to the right to a receiver, Love Jefferson, who pitched it to the running back, Jason Clayton, who had swung out wide—a hook and lateral play. Clayton was tackled in bounds at the twenty-six yard line with just two seconds left, but the clock stopped after the first down. Leaf gathered his team at the line to spike the ball, and, when he did so, it appeared that there was still a second left on the clock. But the clock went to zero and the referees called the game ended in favor of Michigan. Maybe there should have been a second left on the clock; the point has been debated between rival fan bases for years. Yet spiking the ball was an extremely risky move in any event: the time between the ball and chains being set often takes one second off the clock, and the spike play itself can take another second. Whether or not Washington State should've gotten another shot at the end zone, the better play would've been simply to call another pass play and have Washington State run up and execute it, rather than try to spike the ball for no reason.

And, fourteen years later, the 2012 Rose Bowl would also be effectively decided on the same ill-informed decision to spike the ball that had done in Washington State. Wisconsin, trailing Oregon 45–38, tried to spike the ball with two seconds left on the clock. By the time quarterback Russell Wilson had completed the spike play, the clock had run out, and Oregon was victorious. The better tactic would've been to simply call a play than to try to both line up for the spike play and then to run a play thereafter, all within two seconds. Again, as Coach Smith says, the spike play "consumes a second that might have otherwise allowed you an additional play"—this lesson is not only true, it is also painful to learn.

But the most important reason to not spike the ball is that you lose something (depending on the circumstances) even more important than a few seconds: a down, better thought of as an additional chance to score. To illustrate, Smith uses this example: "In 2002 against Auburn, Georgia threw for the end zone four times and hit the fourth one for a touchdown and a victory. They scored with the down that so often gets used up with a spike." The upshot of all this is simple: "These experiences suggest how important this stuff is." And there is no excuse for not having the ability to run another play—if the verbiage required to call a play is too much for just a couple of seconds, then the problem is the verbiage and it must be fixed. Games are lost all too often for the failure to adapt.

So when does spiking the ball make sense? In college football, at least, there really is but one answer: if you are out of timeouts, spiking the ball allows you to get your field goal personnel onto the field for what Coach Smith calls "an unhurried kick." (In the AFC championship game this past NFL season, the Baltimore Ravens rushed their kicker onto the field for a potential game-tying field goal without spiking the ball or calling a timeout. The kicker sprinted onto the field and, having barely any time to get set up, promptly missed the kick and therefore sending the Patriots to the Super Bowl.)

Obviously, a good amount of this analysis depends on the feature in college football that the clock temporarily stops after the offense gains a first down while the first-down chains are reset. In the NFL, where this rule doesn't exist, there are a few more circumstances where a spike may be necessary. Moreover, if the quarterback is sacked by the opponents as the seconds wane, the offense is often forced to spike the ball as there is not enough time to communicate a legal formation and play to receivers who have sprinted far downfield, and this really is the fastest option. (It is also another reason why it is inexcusable and disastrous for a quarterback to give up a sack that late in the game; he simply must throw the ball away.) But the bottom line remains: the spike should be an ancillary option, forced on the offense only when there are no other alternatives. All too often, however, teams unthinkingly sprint up to the line and spike the ball as if that was the proper—no, the only—course. That is extremely dangerous behavior, no matter what the announcers say.

Of course, whether to spike the ball is not an isolated late-game decision, as there are other aspects to managing the clock late in games. The biggest of these might be in the use (and misuse) of timeouts. It's another bit of misguided announcer wisdom that one should not take timeouts into the locker room. Why not? The reason why not is you want to save the timeouts for when you really need them. Remember, if you are efficient at communicating the next play from a no-huddle environment, then timeouts are not very advantageous, saving, at most, a second or so, while giving up something potentially game deciding: the timeout itself. (Note that this is where the analysis can differ markedly for the NFL and college football, as in college the clock stops from the end of a play that garnered a first down while the chains are reset, so the offense can quickly run the next play. In the NFL, by contrast, the clock continues to run while all the players run forward to get set, so a timeout may save more like ten to twenty seconds. Spiking the ball still remains a poor idea in this circumstance even if the clock continues running, as again it shouldn't take any more time to get to the line to run a real play as it would to spike the ball.)

Instead, timeouts are primarily useful in two circumstances: (1) if one gets a first-and-goal inside the ten-yard line, one wants all of his timeouts to run the ball up to three times before kicking, rather than being otherwise forced to pass into the end zone (rather than in front of the goal line as well) and (2) if one is behind and needs two scores, one want to save timeouts to use while the opponent has the ball and is trying to burn time. As Coach Smith put it, "A smart team will often take a lot of timeouts to the locker room."

Many of the analytical issues with all of this arise from thinking of it as the two-minute offense or two-minute drill. Instead, roughly 90 percent of the issues arise within the final thirty seconds of a half or game. The upshot is that while in those last thirty seconds there are a number of variables—including time, timeouts, potential play calls, field position, and the score—additional tricks like calling two plays in the huddle to run on successive plays are unnecessary. One can execute a play, hand signal another one while the referees are getting the ball ready, and snap the ball as soon as one would have if they'd already called a play.

Lastly, play calling late in games is of extreme importance. Many coaches advocate sticking to a base-play approach, where you only call plays that your team is very familiar with; the great Bill Walsh advocated this, and it is sound advice. But as time wanes down, the approach must vary slightly, particularly because defenses are not stupid. You might call plays designed to get to the sideline or past the first-down marker, but your base plays are going to have check downs, and it is potentially very destructive for your quarterback to throw the ball to these otherwise open receivers, especially when your only chance of winning is to throw the ball past the first-down marker and then spike the ball to get a field goal off or to throw it into the end zone.

In other words, how many times have you seen a late-game drive destroyed because the quarterback keeps dumping it off to running backs and underneath receivers and therefore wasting too much time? The philosophy must change: instead of incrementally moving the ball and looking for a high-pass percentage, the better approach is to give the offense four shots to throw a pass of ten yards or more (if the defense decides to bring an all-out blitz of some kind, it's possible to vary the strategy slightly assuming the receiver will be able to catch and run). In the final moments of a game, this is the more efficient use of time. And, of course, a quarterback much be coached to appreciate that he must progress through his receivers differently late in games—as he may only throw passes near the sideline or past ten yards—because sometimes a completed pass is worse than an incomplete one.

There are many other variables that factor into in-game and particularly late-game decision making. And these pressurized moments are among the worst times to try to guess at the proper course. The only way to be good at late-game situations is to think about these issues ahead of time, practice them, and then hope to hell you don't have to use them on game day. But if you do, at least you'll know what you're doing.

TOM BRADY AND THE PATRIOTS SHOW HOW (AND WHY) THE NO-HUDDLE WORKS

SPRING 2012

Tom Brady is a fortunate guy. At this point in his career, a fourth Super Bowl win seems like cosmic overkill: he already has three championship rings, he's a lock for the Hall of Fame, and he's married to a supermodel who's nearly a billionaire on her own. At the same time, it's impossible not to admire his on-field ability. Brady has crafted himself into the perfect NFL quarterback—accurate, smart, and in complete control at all times. In an era when NFL defenses are more complicated than ever, Brady instantly processes the information thrown at him on every play—Who's rushing me? Who's dropping back? What coverage are they in?—and translates it into action.

How is Brady so good at what he does? Much of it has to do with experience and repetition: he's been throwing passes in the NFL for a long time, with many of the same guys blocking for him, to many of the same targets. Brady isn't so much thinking about what he's doing on the field as he is simply filtering repeated scenarios through a brain made expert over time.

Having Bill Belichick as his coach has helped Brady become that expert. But the two of them have had another key advantage this season, one popular at the lower levels of football and now making a resurgence in the NFL: the up-tempo, no-huddle offense. Modern defenses want to match offenses in terms of strength and speed via personnel substitutions. They also want to confuse offenses with movement and disguise. The up-tempo no-huddle stymies those defensive options. The defense doesn't have time to substitute, and it's also forced to show its hand: it can't disguise or shift because the quarterback can snap the ball and take advantage of obvious, structural weaknesses. And when the defense is forced to reveal itself, Tom Brady can change into a better play. The upshot of this tactic: Brady, of all people, sees defenses that are simpler than those most other NFL quarterbacks go up against.

Lots of teams, including the New York Giants, who the Patriots will face in the upcoming Super Bowl, also use the no-huddle offense in certain situations. But nobody in the NFL this season deployed the no-huddle more often and more effectively than the Patriots. Given Brady's success this season—not to mention the success of Peyton Manning's no-huddle Colts in past years—I expect the no-huddle offense to continue its resurgence. It's worth pondering, though, why NFL teams have been slow to incorporate something that seems intuitively to be so much better than the alternatives. Real-life huddles are not nearly as interesting as they are in sports movies, where players frequently debate, bicker, or deliver monologues, somehow within the strict confines of the play clock. In real life, the only thing typically said in the huddle is the play call itself. This is part of the problem: in the NFL, these calls are absurdly long. With only eleven players on a side, there is really no reason other than inertia for there to be lengthy, polysyllabic bits of code to convey each player's assignment. But if that's how playbooks are written, then you really can't go no-huddle; it's impossible to shout "Scatter-Two Bunch-Right-Zip-Fire 22 Z-In

Right-273-H-Pivot-F Flat" to a bunch of people scattered across the width of the field.

But led by Brady, things are changing. Almost all of the information in the aforementioned play call can be shortened to just a few words or numbers, or the relevant information can be conveyed to just the right people: tell the receivers their assignment, the linemen theirs, and so on. And this is increasingly a necessity given the complexity of defenses: it's a lot easier to complete passes when you have a coherent idea of what the defense is doing. It's this defensive movement that's the difference between quarterbacking in college and the NFL. Pro and college teams run the same coverages and blitzes. There are just exponentially more disguises and variations in the NFL.

None of this is particularly new. In the 1980s and early 1990s, both the Cincinnati Bengals and the Buffalo Bills used the no-huddle extensively, and college and high school teams have increasingly moved to no-huddle approaches over the last decade. In his 1997 book *Finding the Winning Edge*, Hall of Fame coach Bill Walsh—whose West Coast offense fueled the growth of complex play calls—predicted that no-huddle offenses using "one word" play calls would come to dominate football. Walsh may have been a bit early, but Brady and Belichick are making his prediction come true.

Then again, while the NFL is a copycat league, not all things are so easily copied. Brady is the perfect no-huddle triggerman, given his experience and ability to process information quickly and efficiently. And few coaches in the NFL are willing to commit to the philosophy as Belichick has. One of the downsides of the no-huddle is that the offense, like the defense, is unable to substitute. NFL coaches love their toys, and they spend a lot of time trying to outsmart each other by creating specific matchups. Belichick, by contrast, values versatility, and he has personnel—particularly his two tight ends, Rob Gronkowski and Aaron Hernandez—that allow him to be flexible. Gronkowski, if he's healthy, is a tremendous threat given his ability to decimate defenders on pass plays and as a run blocker. Hernandez, meanwhile, has recently added running the ball from the backfield to his typical repertoire of pass routes.

Belichick's use of Hernandez as a running back is the best example of how the Patriots outflank defenses. With no traditional runner in the game, Belichick can force the defense to substitute to an anti-zero-running-back personnel grouping. Once they're in this pass-centric setup, Belichick can run the ball with Hernandez anyway. If the defense fails to react, the Patriots can drop back and run a pass play. And they can do this all with or without a huddle, and Brady can figure out his next move within seconds, on the fly. This is why opposing defenses hate facing the Patriots' offense. If the Giants win the Super Bowl, they'll have earned their rings.

PART IV

CONCEPTS

Daring ideas are like chessmen moved forward: they may be beaten, but they may start a winning game.

—Goethe

NICK SABAN'S DEFENSE SCHOOL

FALL 2008

Alabama head coach Nick Saban has been coaching defense—and coaching it quite well—for decades. But there is no question that the defining period of his coaching career was 1991–94, when he was Bill Belichick's defensive coordinator with the Cleveland Browns. Belichick, of course, is the multiple Super Bowl winning head coach of the New England Patriots. And just knowing that Saban was Belichick's pupil tells you a great deal about Saban's defense: he (primarily) bases out of a 3–4 defense (though he can also go to a 4-3); he's very aggressive, especially on passing downs; he wants to stop the run on first and second down; he's not afraid to mix up schemes, coverages, blitzes, and looks of all kinds; and, most importantly, he is intense and attentive to detail—a hallmark of any great coach. Let's allow Saban to explain his defensive philosophy in his own words, from his Louisiana State defensive playbook:

> [Our] philosophy on first and second down is to stop the run and play good zone pass defense. We will occasionally play man-to-man and blitz in this situation. On third down, we will primarily play man-to-man and mix-in some zone and blitzes. We will rush four or more players versus the pass about ninety-percent of the time.
>
> In all situations, we will defend the inside or middle of the field first—defend inside to outside. Against the run, we will not allow the ball to be run inside. We

want to force the ball outside. Against the pass, we will not allow the ball to be thrown deep down the middle or inside. We want to force the ball to be thrown short and/or outside.

...Finally, our job is to take the ball away from the opponents' offense and score or set up good field position for our offense. We must knock the ball loose, force mistakes, and cause turnovers. Turnovers and making big plays win games. We will be alert and aggressive and take advantage of every opportunity to come up with the ball ... The trademark of our defense will be effort, toughness, and no mental mistakes regarding score or situation in any game.

None of this is revolutionary, and much of it is coach patois (there is another section in his playbook where every position is required to put in "super human effort" or else the player is deemed to have failed), but it's a good place to start. Most good defenses begin with the premise that, to be successful, they must stop the run on first and second down to force known passing situations on third down. (Which is one reason why Bill Walsh, the legendary former coach of the San Francisco 49ers—in words far too often unheeded—advocated doing much of one's drop back passing on first down.)

So let's get a bit more specific. Saban's favorite defense is known as "Cover 1 Robber," and it is probably the most common defense in the Southeastern Conference. Basic Cover 1 is quite simple: the "1" refers to a deep safety who aligns in the middle while the offense's potential receivers are covered man-to-man, often with a press or bump-and-run technique. The defense needs a great center fielder at free safety who can stop the deep ball and cover sideline to sideline.

The nice thing about this defense is that it is simple, and, once you've locked in five guys in man coverage along with a deep free safety, you can do whatever you want with the other five defenders. And, maybe most importantly, with just one free safety deep, the defense can get in a lot of eight-man fronts—extra guys to overpower a team's running game. On downs where it is likely that the offense must throw the ball, such as third and long, the defense can find ways to creatively blitz five and have a deep safety, all the

87

while still accounting for all five of the offense's potential receivers with man coverage. That's a basic Cover 1.

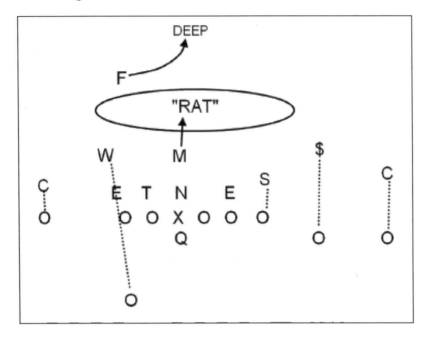

Cover 1 Robber works the same, except there are only four rushers and, along with the deep middle safety, another defender sits at an intermediate level reading the quarterback's eyes to "rob" any pass routes over the middle, such as curls, in routes, and crossing routes. *Robber* is the most popular term for this technique, but Saban's is *Rat*. (I was always partial to the word Homer Smith, the former Alabama and UCLA offensive coordinator, used: *floaters*, a far more descriptive term.) There's nothing magic about this coverage; every NFL team, most BCS teams and many high schools each use it. Indeed, despite all the bluster about "Tampa Two" and other two deep coverages in the NFL, on first and second down most teams run an awful lot of Cover 1 and Cover 1 Robber. The key is for the floater to be able to read run, screen, or pass and to use his eyes to get to the receiver and the ball. It's particularly effective nowadays with the increased use of spread formations,

which most offenses use to open up passing lanes over the middle. Rat players can stop these inside passes and make game-changing interceptions. Cover 1 Robber is useful—though not perfect—against spread offense teams with mobile quarterbacks because the floater may not only read the quarterback's eyes on passing downs but also to watch him for scrambles and to mirror him on run plays.

Another common tactic in Saban's arsenal is the zone blitz. He will go to the zone blitz in passing situations as well as when he feels like he can use it to attack an expected run and still play zone behind it. For example, if a team likes to run off tackle to the tight-end side on a particular down and distance, Saban might call a blitz that attacks that area; the zone blitz lets him still play sound, relatively conservative, coverage behind it. And, like most modern defenses, Saban's most common coverage behind a zone blitz is a 3–3, or three-deep and three-intermediate coverage behind those five blitzing rushers.

The thing to remember is that, for years, when a team blitzed it was playing either Cover 1 or Cover 0 man (or left open spots in its zones), and quarterbacks were coached to throw the ball where the blitzer had come from. What the zone blitz does is allow the defense as a whole to stay in zone coverage; as a result, a quarterback's attempt to throw "hot routes," or adjustments routes to the spot where a blitz came from, will come up empty as a zone-dropping defender that was not expected to be there knifes into the area and intercepts the ball. This is how zone blitzes cause confusion.

Now, some specific coverage techniques used by these coverage players. We should all remember that Saban was a defensive backs coach under Belichick and that is still the position he focuses most on. The first technique Saban implements is having to have his cornerbacks—the outside pass defenders—adjust their leverage on a receiver based on the receiver's split from the ball to the sideline. The theory is that if the wide receiver has cut his split down he is doing one of two things: giving himself more room to run an out-breaking route or cheating in to run a crossing or deep in-breaking route. Thus if the receiver cheats his split in, Saban has his cornerbacks align outside the receiver to defend the out-breaking route because if he runs inside, someone else will be responsible for picking up that receiver in coverage. Similarly, if the receiver lines up very wide, he has given himself room to run an in-breaking route such as a slant. So the cornerback will align inside the receiver to take that route away on the belief that a throw to an out-breaking wide receiver from that far will be a very difficult throw for the quarterback to make. To coach this, Saban uses an imaginary divider line where they believe the receiver's tendencies change to reflect one of the aforementioned two strategies. This line is determined on the basis of scouting the offense.

More significant, however, is that Saban focuses a lot of his teaching on pattern reading within his zone drops. The two zone-dropping schools of thought are to teach spot drops or pattern reading. One can overemphasize the distinction, but, generally, spot dropping was the traditional approach. In this technique, if your outside linebacker was responsible for the weak flat, he would essentially (there is slightly more to it), upon identifying pass, run to a spot on the field and then simply react to the quarterback's eyes and the flight of the ball. A big advantage with spot dropping is that it is easy to teach: if you spend hours with your run-stuffing linebacker on how to attack run plays, you can teach him pass defense in a matter of minutes. But the weakness is that well-coached receivers can become excellent at settling in the holes in the zones between defenders. And, with good receivers and good quarterbacks, modern offenses have become more and more adept at finding and exploiting these open spaces.

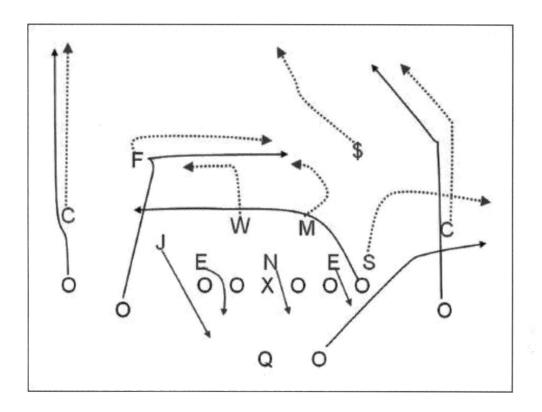

Pattern reading, on the other hand, is much like a matchup zone in basketball. Defenders are responsible for zones, but they play tight to the receivers who come through those zones. Moreover, pattern-read teams begin by immediately coaching their defenders on how to recognize popular pass route combinations (and indeed, the very concept of pass combinations themselves) and each week zero in on the five to fifteen most common pass concepts they will see from that opponent. When performed correctly, pattern-reading defenders know exactly how to cover receivers in their zones and seamlessly (in a quite literal sense) pass the receivers onto other defenders as they run their routes. Saban further distinguishes his defenses in that he uses pattern reading in almost all of his coverages, including the traditional Cover 3 or three-deep coverage, whereas many coaches only let certain defenders pattern read or only use it with certain defenses. Instead, Saban demands perfection and has no qualms about spending the grinding hours working on the finer details to make it happen. Sounds a lot like Belichick, no? There's a reason both of them win a lot of championships.

THE LONG ARC OF STEVE SPURRIER

FALL 2009

In the 1990s, Steve Spurrier was the King of Offense. He passed—no, blitzkrieged may be more accurate—and wisecracked his way to SEC title after SEC title and a national championship as head coach of the University of Florida. Danny Wuerffel, Spurrier's quarterback for much of his great stretch at Florida, became the original Heisman-winning Gator quarterback/pious Christian, and he made stars of receivers as diverse as Reidel Anthony, Ike Hilliard, Jack Jackson, Chris Doering, and Travis McGriff. But all that was more than a decade ago.

Spurrier left for the NFL, and he did not exactly set the world on fire there, to say the least, and his tenure as Ol' Ball Coach in Chief at South Carolina has been uneven. Strangely, too, when he has had success at South Carolina it has been with significant help from his defenses, which is surprising for someone known for revolutionizing how offense was played in the South. But regardless of how Spurrier's offense has performed in recent seasons, it's worth reflecting on how his schemes propelled his Gators into the national elite; how his offense, for a time at least, was the best in the land.

Upon taking the job at South Carolina, Spurrier explained to *Sports Illustrated* what made his offense go: "It's a style of offense that uses a lot of draw plays and play-action off that," he said. "We try to audible more than some people. A lot of times our quarterbacks are reading coverages and searching for the best play."

This was a very honest answer, so let's unpack it. At Duke and Florida, Steve's offenses were based on a triumvirate of simple but well-put-together concepts that put defensive players in an extreme bind: the dropback pass, the lead draw play, and the play-action off of a fake lead-draw. Spurrier began with the basic drop back pass—the five-step or seven-step drop and throw. He preferred then, as he does now, deeper drops simply because he liked to throw it further down the field, and the deep drops times up with deep pass patterns by receivers. And so the first look Spurrier gave an opposing defense was the quarterback dropping straight back while the line pass blocked.

When he looked to run it, however, he managed to simulate the same deep drop with the lead draw. This play works just like it sounds: the quarterback retreats like he is going to pass and then hands it off to a running back who has mimicked a pass-blocking motion before receipt of the football. Usually a fullback or tight end acted as a lead blocker. Even more important than the quarterback's drop back action was the action of the offensive line: because it was a draw, the offensive tackles showed a pass block and let the defensive ends run upfield. The offensive line's job was to make sure the ends couldn't get inside to disrupt the inside run play. The interior linemen initially showed a pass-block look before attacking the interior of the defense. As simple as it was, Spurrier's running backs (many of whom went on to become NFL starters), including Errict Rhett, Fred Taylor, and Earnest Graham, racked up a lot of yards on this play.

And then, the final twist of the knife: the play-action pass off of the lead draw, where Spurrier got his big plays. On Steve's preferred lead draw play action, his quarterback began his drop back like a pass drop, faked the draw handoff, and then popped up to look downfield for his receivers. Again, though, it's the line that is so important. As former San Francisco 49ers head coach Bill Walsh once explained—and as Spurrier acutely understood—play action from the lead draw is maybe the best play-action pass of all because the linemen pass block; there is no fear that they will give away the play's intent by showing pass too early. Together, these three concepts allowed Spurrier's offense to throw the ball down the field, over and over again, while still controlling the defense's front seven. And, with the extensive use of draws and run fakes, he was able to have additional blockers to protect his quarterback on those deep pass plays.

But this only tells part of the story. The other reason Spurrier's receivers could get so incredibly wide open—and also why his offense literally could not "turn off" when his teams were drubbing some sacrificial lamb at the Swamp—was that he gave his receivers the freedom to adjust their routes on the fly. His favorite play is known in his system as Ralph (to the right) or Lonnie (to the left).

(Incidentally, Spurrier's system far and away wins the prize for best play names. In the football world, where play names are notable only for their descriptiveness—such as Z shallow cross—or their pedantry—any polysyllabic NFL play call—Spurrier's play names—Biddle, Corkers, Righty/Lefty, Ralph/Lonnie, Mills, Bopper, Wheelies, and, of course, Steamers—are refreshing.) Below is an image of Lonnie, drawn in Spurrier's own handwriting, against Cover 3 and Cover 2.

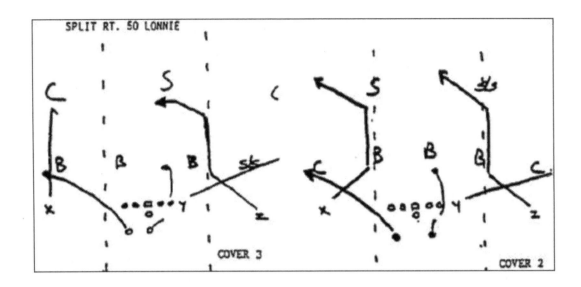

SPLIT RT. 50 LONNIE

COVER 3

COVER 2

Spurrier gave his two outside receivers the ability to adjust their routes based on the coverage they saw. On the backside, the receiver either ran a deep square-in at fifteen yards or a deep post route down the middle. The receiver ran the post if the defense left the middle of the field open—i.e., two split safeties, each on the hash, in a two-deep zone with no one in the middle of the field—or the deep fifteen-yard square-in if the defense had a deep middle safety who would take the post away. But the primary route was on the front side, to the left in Lonnie and the right in Ralph. This receiver could run either a corner route or a curl route, depending on the coverage. His job was to get a sense of where the cornerback was playing him: if the corner played off and deep to the outside, the receiver would push to fifteen yards and just come back to the quarterback on the curl. If the corner stayed short, the receiver wanted to push inside and then upfield before breaking to the corner.

From the quarterback's perspective, this made perfect sense. The curl route should come open inside the linebacker or flat defender who the inside receiver has occupied by running a route towards the sideline. Against a two-deep look, however, the defense has the flat and inside covered, so Spurrier wanted to put the cornerback in a bind by putting one guy in front of him and another behind him—a high-to-low read.

In this way, his offense was always right: you play him in Cover 2, he throws the corner, you play him in Cover 3, he throws the curl. If you blitz, then his quarterback was responsible for seeing that and audibling the play to a quick pass or quick screen—or throwing the deep post to the backside wide receiver. When all this worked, it was beautiful. Indeed, one of the greatest offensive performances I've ever seen came in the 1995 Florida–Tennessee game, where Spurrier's team scored 48 unanswered points after trailing by double digits to beat a Peyton Manning–led UT, 62–37. Danny Wuerffel had six touchdown passes, with the majority of his yards and all of his touchdowns coming on just a few plays. One was Ralph/Lonnie, which Spurrier used to ignite the rally by throwing curls when UT backed off and corner routes for touchdowns when they went to Cover 2. The second was the simple smash pattern against Tennessee's Cover 2 defense, where the outside receiver runs a five-yard hitch and the inside receiver runs a corner route behind him—the same high-to-low read as with Lonnie, but with the receivers' roles switched. Tennessee then tried to switch to Cover 4, or quarters coverage, and Spurrier called his Mills concept (where an outside receiver runs a post route behind an inside receiver that ran an in-breaking route to suck up the safeties). Not too bad if you can hang 62 on a big SEC rival using essentially three pass plays.

And yet, as great as it was, it's clear Spurrier's offense is not nearly as explosive now as it used to be. This is not to take away from his success now—indeed, it may show evolution on Spurrier's part that he can win games without throwing for 400 yards—but sometimes it's hard to believe he's using the same scheme that once put up all of those points. There are plenty of reasons for this that have nothing to do with Xs and Os, of course, but the scheme is not wholly innocent. Indeed, others have adopted many of Steve's best schematic innovations, so they are no longer that innovative.

And his offense, after initially resisting change, has begun to undergo it, but without a clear direction, stealing a few concepts from here and a few more from there. This hurts him in the passing game because he asks his quarterbacks to make a lot of difficult throws from deep drops, thus exposing them to hits and missed reads. But as he has added pass protectors to protect his quarterback—Spurrier was famously blitzed right out of the NFL—he has lost some of the variability and explosiveness that made his passing game at Florida so good.

At core, Spurrier's system is still great—it's still well designed, as it is based on core concepts meshed with sensible fakes and counters, and giving players freedom to succeed will never go out of style. Yet while others have passed Spurrier in terms of innovation, that was always inevitable. Of course, it's not all about innovation; football remains about winning. Steve still knows how to do that.

AL BORGES:
MICHIGAN'S MAN IN THE MIDDLE

SUMMER 2011

The word that comes to mind when I think of Al Borges, the Michigan offensive coordinator under new coach Brady Hoke, is *solid*. Solid isn't inspirational, but, in Borges's it's been enough to win football games and put up points. And, if nothing else, this fits new head coach Brady Hoke's mantra: style points are irrelevant if we win.

In football, play callers and game plan designers are typically governed by the adage of the elder Oliver Wendell Holmes Sr., who (possibly apocryphally) observed that "a man's mind, once shaped by an idea, never again regains its original dimensions." In this way, Borges, who is older than Rich Rodriguez, is not unlike the outgoing Michigan coach. But if Rodriguez's mind became enamored with the spread offense and its possibilities—and every plan he put together was through that lens—Borges too is a lifelong student of the hot offense of his youthful coaching days: the West Coast offense of Bill Walsh and his many disciples.

Borges, who first became an offensive coordinator at Portland State in 1986, spent his most formative (and notable) years in the Pac-10 from 1995 through 2000, for one season with Oregon and the latter five with UCLA under Bob Toledo. During that stretch,

Borges's offense showcased all of the latest strategic technology of the age, from screens off play-action looks to five- and seven-step drops and zone running meshed with a pro-style power game. Borges even coaxed fantastic seasons out of Tony Graziani at Oregon (who had a brief career with the Atlanta Falcons) and Cade McNown, who, aside from being known as a major first-round bust with the Chicago Bears, is probably best known for being banned from the Playboy mansion by Hugh Hefner. Credit goes to Borges for the success he achieved with them.

But Bob Toledo's fortunes at UCLA turned sour after McNown left, and Borges stopped briefly at Cal before spending a couple of seasons at Indiana under Gerry DiNardo. He then made a move to Auburn to coach under Tommy Tuberville. After some success at Auburn with Jason Campbell at quarterback (and with future NFL backs Cadillac Williams and Ronnie Brown sharing the backfield) that eventually declined in later years, he, after a year out of football, teamed with Brady Hoke as offensive coordinator under Hoke at San Diego State. In their first season together in 2009, the Aztec's offense improved in nearly every category, though only marginally so, and, during the 2010 season, San Diego State's offense flourished into a formidable attack, finishing in the top fifteen or twenty in most offensive categories and averaging around thirty-five points a game.

Throughout this long and winding process, Borges—always as offensive coordinator and play caller—has brought his West Coast offense with him. But the important thing is that he has evolved from those Cade McNown days to an offense that looks decidedly more modern than simply a college emulation of the 1995 (or 1985) San Francisco 49ers. At San Diego State, his teams used lots of shotgun, quick passes, some spread offense–style zone read plays, receiver screens, and other gadgets, and he generally did an excellent job of getting his playmakers the ball.

All of that sounds great, if not a bit obvious ("I would hope the offensive coordinator gets the ball to the playmakers"), but the main concern is it leaves aside the one thing Borges has never coached: a mobile, dynamic-with-his-feet quarterback like Denard Robinson. Indeed, in Rich Rodriguez's spread-to-run offense, Robinson wasn't so much a quarterback as he was some kind of pre–World War II halfback, whose job it was to run, throw, fake, and maybe even punt now and again. Under Rich Rodriguez, Robinson *was* Michigan's offense, which began to eschew even the "read" part of zone reads in favor of simply having Robinson keep it himself on an outside zone play, time and time again. So how will Borges use such a dynamic and—in the case of his throwing—raw talent?

No one can say for sure, but the most useful thing to do to answer this question may be to study the passing and running games that Borges has historically used and to consider how Robinson might fit in—or bend the offense to his strengths.

The biggest difference between the Rodriguez system and what Borges brings in is his West Coast offense passing philosophy. In the Rodriguez spread-to-run system, the passing game was designed as a complement to the run game: play action and bubble screens if the outside linebackers or safeties come up for the run, quick passes of five or six yards underneath if the coverage defenders played loose, and simple sprint out and bootleg concepts to get Denard out of the pocket and to throw off a single defender—if the defender takes one receiver, Denard throws it to the other, and vice versa. The point was to make the defense play honest against the pass to open up big running lanes for Robinson and company.

Borges, however, will ask Denard Robinson and his other quarterbacks to do things a bit differently. "West Coast," like "spread offense," is a vague, almost meaningless term, but the Borges offense is built around some different principles than Rodriguez's offense. The "West Coast offense" is the popular term given (by the media, at least) to the pro-style rhythm-passing offense designed by Bill Walsh and perfected with the San Francisco 49ers in the 1980s and early 1990s. This offense was built around quick, ball-control throws to receivers, tight ends, and running backs and was revolutionary for its time in that the pass was the featured part of the offense, rather than the running game. Of course, that looks quaint with the hindsight of the modern era, as some spread-to-pass college teams will throw the ball fifty or sixty times a game, while the West Coast offense was considered heretical for throwing it maybe twenty-five to thirty-five times.

But the West Coast offense is extremely well designed and sound, as evidenced by the many NFL titles won by Walsh and his protégés. And Borges has a great deal of experience distilling the key elements of that pro offense to the college ranks, which gives him an advantage over current pro coaches who have tried to make the transition to college and failed to teach their offense under the strict practice limitations at that level. Among the key elements of the West Coast offense that Borges features, the first is timing. Under Borges, there will be a significantly greater premium put on the timing between quarterbacks and receivers than was previously the case at Michigan. This doesn't mean timing was irrelevant before, but the West Coast offense is built around tying the steps of the quarterbacks and receivers together. For example, let's say Borges calls the curl/flat play, which in Walsh's system was one of the first he installed, calling it "22 Z In." I've drawn it up from a pro set (two wide receivers, a tight end, a halfback, and a fullback), although it can be run from a variety of sets (more on that in a bit).

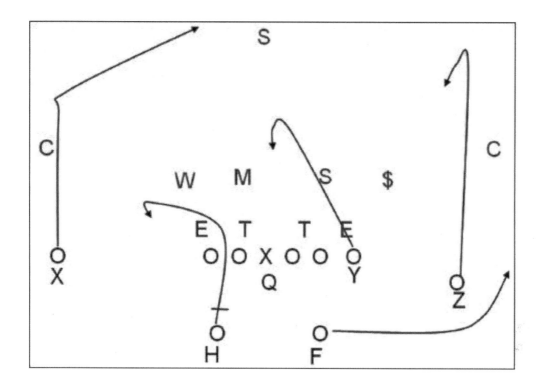

The quarterback takes a five-step drop from under center, which means he retreats backward (with, if he's right-handed, his left shoulder pointing straight down the field so as not to give anything away) for five steps. The first three are known as "big steps" as he tries to get depth. The fourth and fifth steps are shorter steps, referred to as "gather steps," as he needs to come under control to propel his body forward and deliver a pass on target.

The first read in 22 Z-In is the tight end, or *Y* in the diagram. He splits the middle and strong side linebackers and looks to find an open spot at a depth of eight to ten yards, depending on how clean his release is—i.e., whether he is jammed or held up as he releases off the line. What makes this a timing pass concept is that the quarterback is not allowed to drop back, shuffle around, hitch up before throwing to the tight end. Instead, if the tight end is open—or, more accurately, will be open even though he hasn't yet turned around to face the quarterback—the quarterback must deliver the ball as soon as his fifth step hits. One-two-three-four-five—Throw! This cannot be stressed enough, and it is not an easy skill to learn. Imagine having to run backward for several steps immediately before you swing a golf club or shoot a deep three-point shot. But lost steps—and therefore lost time—are not permitted in a timing-based passing scheme like the West Coast offense; the passing windows will close, and the timing with the other receivers will be lost.

If the tight end is covered, however, this means that the interior linebackers have collapsed on him, which should open up passing lanes for other receivers through which the quarterback may be able to deliver the ball. The quarterback will then move on to the second receiver in his progression, the curl route by Z. This time the quarterback does take a hitch-up or gather step, slightly shuffling forward to gain leverage—and to allow a receiver who has run a slightly deeper route to get further downfield. If the passing lane to the curl route is open—which will be because the strong safety ($ in the diagram) has widened to take the fullback (F) on a swing route to the flat—the quarterback will deliver it to the curl. Indeed, the receiver running the curl is not told, "Hey run out there and turn around." He is instead given specific steps as well. Against loose coverage, he runs a seven-step curl: five big, or speed, steps with two gather steps at the end of his route to stop his momentum and bring his body under control; he then turns back to the quarterback and works to find an open window through which the ball can be thrown. If the defense is in man-to-man, the receiver has a bit more freedom but still must get to at least ten or twelve yards, get inside leverage, and do so within the allotted time.

Finally, if the strong safety retreats to take away the curl, the quarterback must, after having taken his gather step, reset his feet to look for the fullback (F) in the flat on the swing route as an outlet pass. And all this must happen within 2.5 seconds. This is what a timing-based passing game is all about.

But wait, there's more. Notice the backside split end (the *X* receiver) on a post route to the deep middle? The quarterback will throw it to him if the safety (*S* in the diagram) moves out of position. This is actually what the quarterback is watching during the first three steps of his drop back. If the deeper pass is there, he finishes his drop and takes it. If not, he must either go through the rest of his progression or, if he has stayed on the post too long, look for his *other* check-down receiver, the halfback, or *H*.

And we're not done yet. What if the defense blitzes? If the inside linebackers (*M* or *S*) rush the quarterback, the read for the quarterback can essentially remain the same—throw it to the tight end over the middle off of five steps with no hitch or gather. But if the strong safety (*$*) blitzes, then the fullback (*F*) is "hot," meaning that the quarterback must now alter his read to throw it to the swing route at the end of his drop without shuffling in the pocket, lest he be killed. This all must be practiced and perfected, of course, but once it is mastered the way those 49ers teams had mastered it, a team can march up and down the field throwing this same concept, and concepts like it, over and over and over again no matter what the defense presents. Timing and play design, along with precise execution, will overcome any problem a defense may present.

But, of course, when one thinks of these timing, ball-control passes with efficient reads, one doesn't think of Denard Robinson. He is many, many wonderful things, whether it is the electrifying specialty guy he was his freshman year or the honest-to-goodness spread offense quarterback he became his sophomore year. Yet isn't it a bit aggressive to ask him now to be Tom Brady?

Yes and no. Robinson should be able to master these skills, but the question is how long will it take—it may take more than one year, and may even take more than two. Much is made of the difference in footwork between pro-style and college shotgun spread offenses, and it is a real challenge, but only in this sense: it's not that the shotgun teaches bad footwork; it's that the point of the shotgun is to *eliminate* a lot of footwork from the equation. Many of Denard's throws under Rich Rodriguez were "catch and throws," and others were action passes where he had choices on the move without any specific timing. This past spring, the Michigan quarterbacks spent an awful lot of their time *thinking*—far too much to be fluid in the offense, which affected their timing and accuracy. This was because everything was new—the footwork, the reads, and even many of the routes and types of throws themselves. Fortunately, Denard Robinson remains dangerous even with diminished passing, and he has two years to develop into a West Coast passer.

But it's almost time for the 2011 season, so what can a prostyle coach like Borges do with all the talent and returning starters he has, though they were trained in the spread offense? Despite his pro-style mentality, Borges has shown some flexibility over the years. I was impressed with how his San Diego State offenses had adapted many of his old concepts to a newer-school approach with a great deal of success (though primarily in his second year as opposed to his first). SDSU featured a variety of one-back sets and zone-running plays to go with Borges' West Coast passing concepts, and many of these too had even been adapted to a spread look.

One example is the venerable "Texas" concept. The play is a West Coast staple, used most famously by Mike Holmgren when he was head coach of the Green Bay Packers to counteract Tony Dungy's vaunted Tampa Two defenses. Traditional Cover 2 features two deep safeties who divide the field into halves, while everyone else plays underneath coverage. The theory of the defense was, first, for the cornerbacks to play tight, press coverage, and jam the outside receivers to prevent them from catching short passes and turning them into long gains and, second, through the help of talented linebackers, to remain effective against the run, particularly outside runs where the cornerbacks acted as force defenders to funnel everything inside and back into the teeth of the defense. The weakness of the defense, however, could be found with play-action, which drew those linebackers up while a tight end or slot receiver ran down the deep middle of the field behind them. Tony Dungy's

Tampa Two defense sought to gain all the advantages of traditional Cover 2 while eliminating the tight end down the middle by simply having the middle linebacker drop to a spot fifteen to eighteen yards downfield. This actually transformed the defense into something of a three-deep defense, though with Cover 2 coverage principles.

Mike Holmgren's response was to run the Texas concept, which is a high/low attack on that middle linebacker who in the Tampa Two is responsible for the deep middle of the field. The tight end would still try to split the safeties and get deep down the middle for a big pass, but the fullback would run an angle route underneath him. On the angle route, the fullback began by running toward the flat (similar to his assignment on 22 Z-In), but he would then plant and angle back inside. If the middle linebacker dropped deep, the quarterback dropped it underneath to the fullback. Eventually, the middle linebacker got tired of giving up six, seven, and eight yard gains over and over and would try to take away that fullback, and—bang—he thus opened the defense up to a big pass play to the tight end. (That is, when Mike Holmgren could convince Brett Favre to be patient and keep throwing it to the fullback rather than forcing it to the tight end too early.)

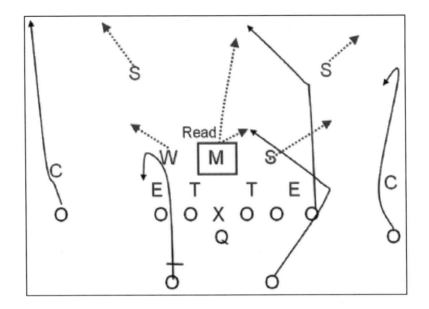

Borges loved this play at UCLA and even at Auburn, but by the time he got to San Diego State, defenses were showing more complex looks and he couldn't get away with simply lining up in the old-school pro set necessary to run the play. So he used a similar concept—a high/low attack of the middle or another inside linebacker—but with some new wrinkles. Indeed, Borges adapted the Texas concept to another pro favorite, Levels, which is essentially the same read.

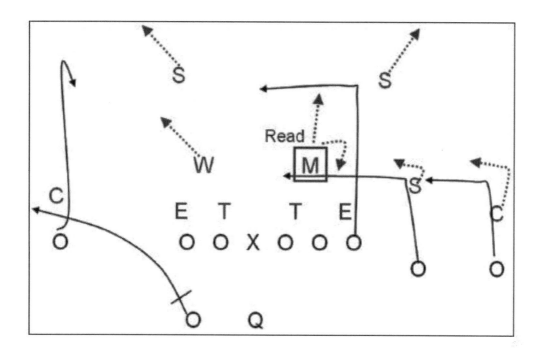

This is a more modern approach—it has been Peyton Manning's favorite play with the Indianapolis Colts for roughly a decade—but gets the offense to the same spot with a different look and different personnel. Note too the backside opportunities: from the three receiver or trips set, the backside has a curl/flat read (the same as 22 Z-In), with the outside receiver running a twelve-yard curl while the running back runs a shoot route. I expect Borges to be able to adapt his pro-style blend attack to something with at least some degree of immediate effectiveness and which will improve over time. For now, he's putting a lot on the quarterbacks to help them learn. When it comes to game time, he will have to scale that back to focus on what they can do well.

But what of the run game? First things first: say goodbye to the pure spread-and-shred approach, but not to the zone read or zone run plays generally. Although Brady Hoke seemed to indicate that the zone was a sissy concept in general and that they would run the Power-O play (which coaches like as much for its name as for its), the data belies that conclusion. In San Diego State's bowl game against Navy, SDSU ran the ball forty-one times. Eleven times they ran the Power-O, and another three they ran a toss scheme, which is an outside play with some similarity to the Power-O. But they ran the inside zone seventeen times (including a zone read!) and the outside zone another two times. So while Hoke might claim that the zone is on its way out, Borges doesn't seem to be calling his games that way.

And all to the better. The Michigan players know how to run the zone play and are quite good at it. But what of the Power-O play? The concept is simple: the offensive line "down blocks," or blocks away from the point of attack to both get leverage and generate double-teams on the defensive tackle. The fullback (or sometimes an H-back or tight end type) kicks out the defensive end, creating an alley for the runner. But the runner's job is to follow the block of his lead blocker, a pulling backside guard.

It's a sound play, and Michigan's players will get better at it. It should serve the job Hoke wants it to do, which is to establish tempo, mind-set, and attitude. Whether it produces results this year is another matter, but Hoke wants to establish a lot of things at Michigan, and, unlike his predecessor (for better or for worse), his focus is not on gaudy yards-per-game averages.

And what of the running quarterback? I can only speculate, but here are my thoughts on how Denard Robinson will be used. First, expect a reduction of called quarterback runs. Michigan's best play last year was the outside zone where Denard Robinson simply took the ball and ran with no fake or read; it was single-wing football brought into the modern age. That play is likely no longer in the playbook, and it must be admitted it resulted in Robinson taking something of a beating over the course of the season. Second, don't be shocked when you see a healthy dose of the zone read even from a supposedly pro-style coach, at least at times. The play is not expensive to install, and it is very simple. What you won't see are the complex cat-and-mouse games Rodriguez engaged in (and ultimately tried to short-circuit by having Robinson take the ball around end) that were designed to counteract "scrape exchange" techniques—i.e., "games" where the defense moved around the defenders the quarterback was supposed to be reading to confuse him—and various other tactics defensive coaches used to mess with the spread-to-run read offenses. This especially became an issue for Rodriguez as everyone from Ohio State to Purdue were using some kind of spread tactics in the Big 10, and so defenses got a lot of practice defending such attacks. The upshot for Borges is that he'll use spread offense concepts, but because he's neither steeped in them nor committed to them, if they stop working, he'll move on to something else, primarily the passing game.

Ultimately, Brady Hoke and Al Borges's first year at Michigan will be about transition. Michigan has had too many of those sorts of seasons recently, but anyone expecting this offense to average forty points a game in the Big 10 (something even Rodriguez didn't do) will be disappointed. Instead, Hoke wants to build a program from the ground up: good (better?) defense, good running, solid passing, and solid characters. The reason Denard Robinson is a good fit for the new offense has less to do with his talent than his character—he will work to become a great player, whatever they ask him to do, even if it is ugly at times. And I'm confident he will become an excellent *quarterback* (as opposed to the all-purpose omniback he has been) but I am not sure it will be this season.

The good news, however, is that so long as the offense doesn't fall off a cliff, any improvement on defense is sure to have a much bigger effect than whatever changes occur on offense. A little help on defense will make Al Borges's job a lot easier.

GUS MALZAHN'S MULTIPLE ATTACK

SUMMER 2011

By now, Gus Malzahn's story is well-known. Malzahn, a high school coach known for his high-scoring offenses and talented players at Springdale, Arkansas, thought he got his big break into big-time college coaching when Houston Nutt hired him to be the offensive coordinator at Arkansas—so long as he brought several of his players and his highly touted quarterback, Mitch Mustain, with him. Malzahn installed his up-tempo no-huddle offense at Arkansas, only to have Nutt junk it after one game, a merciless slaughtering at the hands of the Matt Leinart/Reggie Bush Southern Cal juggernaut in 2005. Arkansas nevertheless went on to have a very successful season, but by the end of the year it was clear that the Malzahn experiment would not be repeated; the personalities did not mesh. And so it appeared that this high school coach had reached his limits and the story was over.

Except that it wasn't. Malzahn took a position as co-offensive coordinator at Tulsa before jumping to become an Auburn Tiger. And, in the four years since he left Arkansas, his offense has finished in the top ten in total offense three times, including first overall in both of his seasons at Tulsa. (The other year, Malzahn's first at Auburn, the Tigers finished 16th in total offense, which still represented a ninety-spot increase from the 106th offensive ranking from the prior year.) And, together with head coach Gene Chizik, quarterback phenom Cam Newton, and the rest of the Auburn staff and players, Gus accomplished something beyond statistics: a dream season that involved multiple comeback wins (including, most gloriously for the Tiger faithful, against the fighting Nick Sabans of Alabama), a Southeastern Conference championship, and, finally, a National Championship. Not bad for a high school coach.

Cam Newton, of course, deserves much of the credit for the Tigers' potent offense in 2010. Although his immense physical talents were apparent immediately, his ability to read defenses and understand the concepts Gus presented was an extremely pleasant surprise. And most surprising of all was Newton's impressive leadership of his team in the heat of battle—in overtime against Clemson, in comeback wins over South Carolina and Kentucky, in hard-fought SEC battles against LSU and Mississippi State, and, of course, on the road at Alabama. The fruits of this effort were apparent (if they weren't already) in the SEC championship game rematch against South Carolina and in the resiliency shown in gutting out the championship against Oregon, a team that, like Auburn, had earned the right to be there and didn't want to go home a loser, but did.

All of this is a credit to Cam Newton, but it also is a credit to the simplicity and precision of Malzahn's system. Newton was an incredible talent, but he was also a junior college transfer from Blinn College who suddenly had to chair a no-huddle, on-the-fly offense in the thick of the SEC—the kind of thing that can go horrendously wrong unless your coaches put you in position to succeed. The framework of Gus's offense is built on the idea that it will all be called from the no-huddle, so there is no room for extraneous verbiage (as there is with long, never-ending NFL play calls), and the premium is on players' playing the game: "If you're thinking you're not playing," is a common refrain of Malzahn's.

To do this, Gus has had to evolve over time. One of the interesting changes in Gus's reputation was his evolution from being known as a pass-happy throw-it-all-the-time coach to a run-first one.

Auburn's offense last season might have been spread and no-huddle, but it was, at core, a power-based offense. While at Springdale, Malzahn was known for his passing yards, and at Tulsa, quarterback Paul Smith threw for over five thousand yards in 2007. Coaches study Malzahn's offense now, however, for how he designs and puts together his running game as they do for any spread passing elements.

The foundation of Malzahn's running game is the Power-O play. It's not a new or fancy scheme—if you go to the famous "C.O.O.L. clinic," the veteran offensive line coaches there refer to it as "God's play"—and it is extremely popular at every level of football, from high school to the NFL. Power, in its base form, is simple. The play side of the line—where the runner is going to—blocks down, meaning the offensive tackle does not block the defensive end but instead double-teams the defenders inside of him to crush them, get movement, and create a wall of blockers to cut off the backside. The hole for the runner is created by the fullback, who "kicks out" the defensive end. While the kick out is not an easy block, it also doesn't have to be a pancake: all the fullback needs to do is seal off the defender to the outside. The runner bursts through the hole, but not without some assistance, as he follows the backside offensive guard (who lines up just to the center's left), who is pulling to lead the way as a blocker on the strong side linebacker. The running back is instructed to follow the guard and to cut off his block, meaning to run right behind him and use his block as a shield to spring him into the secondary.

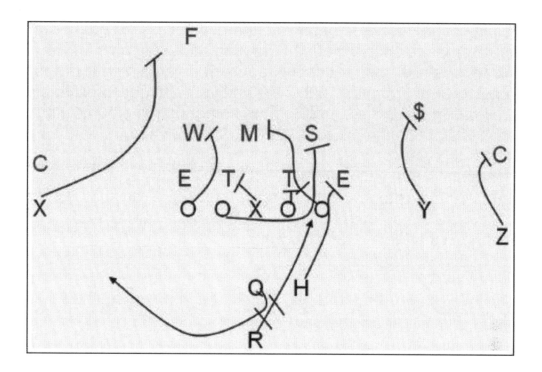

This is just the kind of base run play that Malzahn likes: adaptable, flexible, and powerful. The downhill, forceful nature of the scheme is crucial, but so is its adaptability. Indeed, while the play drawn here shows it being run by a traditional running back, who was Auburn's best inside runner in 2010? Cam Newton, the quarterback. Through just a few slight variations, Malzahn found a way to combine this power blocking with an option play, all through his uncanny knack for putting players in position to succeed via one of the great spread offense wrinkles of the last few years: the inverted veer.

The traditional veer is one of the oldest option plays. The traditional veer involves having the running back run inside while the quarterback reads a down lineman just like the quarterback chooses who will keep the ball. If the defender the quarterback is reading tries to tackle the running back, the quarterback pulls the ball from him and steps around (sometimes with an additional pitch read for a full triple option). If the defender sits there watching the quarterback, the quarterback hands it off to the running back who runs inside. Think about those great wishbone teams from the old days or the Nebraska teams from the 1990s: they hit you with option pitches and quarterback runs until—suddenly, and somehow—the burly fullback blasted straight up the middle for a fifty-yard touchdown, untouched. That was the veer.

Malzahn's innovation (to be fair, the first team I saw do this was TCU in 2009) was to invert the veer by having the running back run outside while the quarterback became the inside threat. And Malzahn did it all with power blocking.

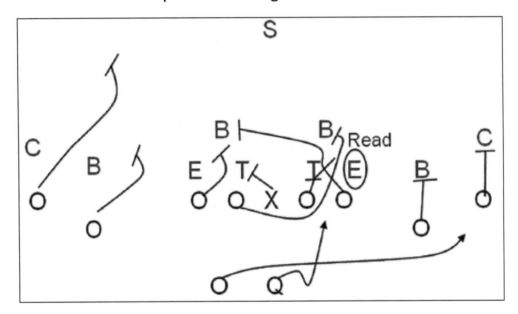

As the diagram shows, the only difference in terms of blocking is the removal of the fullback blocking the defensive end, which is now unnecessary because the quarterback "blocks" him by reading him—by making him wrong no matter what he does. The rest is the same: the play side of the line blocks down while the backside guard pulls and leads up to the linebacker.

Now, with the changed backfield action, the running back—typically a speedy runner like Onterio McCalebb—runs laterally past the quarterback to threaten a wide sweep. The quarterback reads the defensive end: if he fails to widen for the sweep (as he must to account for the speed of the running back around end), it's a simple handoff sweep around end. But if he does widen, then the quarterback pulls the ball back and shoots up inside, now acting as the running back and cutting off the block of the backside guard. This was probably Auburn's best play with Cam Newton; indeed, almost all of Newton's big runs (including electrifying ones against South Carolina and LSU) came on this play, especially as Newton learned to cut it back after getting into the thick of the defense. Moreover, Gus often called the same play on the goal line but used multiple tight ends and a power formation instead of a spread four-wide receiver set. Newton typically either knifed through the defense or simply leaped over the pile and into the end zone.

Obviously, the play works best when the quarterback is not only a good runner, but a dynamic *inside* runner. But it's not all about one play, it's about adapting scheme to players. Sometimes, the talent and competition are such that there aren't many options, but most of the time, it's all about making the most of what you have.

These are traits that go back to Gus's high school days. As Malzahn explained to *Sports Illustrated* before the BCS title game last fall, when he was promoted from defensive coordinator (!) to head coach at Hughes High School in Arkansas in the early '90s, he bought the book *The Delaware Wing-T: An Order of Football*, by Harold "Tubby" Raymond—the book is a coaching classic—and "went by it word-for-word." The book described the Delaware wing-t in ways any coach could understand and install, and, despite being a classic, almost historical work, it was the perfect training for modern football. The wing-t was one of the oldest and best offenses for a long, long time, and the Delaware spin was put on the offense by Tubby Raymond. The offense is built around misdirection, leverage, angles, and fakes and is designed to spread the ball around among the various offensive players and to use them each in ways to maximize their talents. Sound familiar? It's mere detail that the offense was under center and used two true running backs and a halfback rather than the multiple formations, shotgun, and multiple receivers Malzahn would come to favor.

Malzahn ran the Delaware wing-t, essentially unchanged, for years until the spread offense arose. As the spread came in, Malzahn married his traditional wing-t concepts with the nouveau spread, and the results were devastating for defenses. And later, at the college level, he did much the same thing at Tulsa as he merged his offense with the one brought in by co-offensive coordinator Herb Hand, a spread offense disciple of Rich Rodriguez who now coaches at Vanderbilt.

But despite the evolutions, many of Gus's best plays still find their roots in the wing-t. Power and its various adaptations have wing-t ties, and, even more directly, since he was at Springdale, Malzahn has been running a version of the old wing-t buck sweep, albeit from the shotgun. Most teams don't use this because it's a kind of slow-developing play to the outside, but Herb Hand once mentioned that it averaged more than ten yards an attempt at Tulsa for a full season. And for Tigers fans, the evidence is even more immediate: In 2009, Ben Tate racked up over 1,300 yards rushing, many of them on this very play.

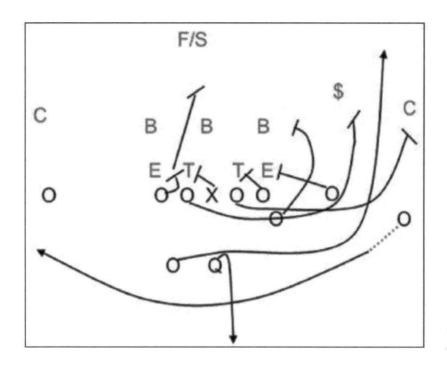

The buck, or hand sweep, is classic wing-t: the line, tight ends, and receivers all block down, or step to their inside to get an angle to cut off the defenders' pursuit, while both guards pull and lead to the outside. Note that it's not that different from the Power-O play previously described: the line still blocks down and there are play side pulling guards leading the way. One difference is that the slot receiver blocks down as well, and he effectively takes the place of the fullback on the kick-out in power except now the assignment is to seal that defender to the inside. Hopefully (for the offense) the defender never sees the slot receiver before the block, resulting in a pancake.

Meanwhile, the quarterback executes a fake, causing the defense to hesitate for just a moment, and off the runner goes. And if the generic buck sweep is classic wing-t, the Auburn version is classic Malzahn, an age-old concept combined not just with the shotgun but with a funky formation and receiver motion behind the quarterback and running back. And, of course, there are variations off this one play. As always with Gus, he has counters to the counter, and the play-action pass off this play is deadly—the wing-t with spread offense flavors.

When not throwing screens or play-action bombs, Malzahn does have a sophisticated if streamlined passing offense. With simple throws that complement his running game, Malzahn's system is quarterback friendly. But the biggest advantage a young quarterback has when playing for Gus Malzahn is the real foundation of his offense, the tempo. The schemes are important, of course, but Malzahn cares primarily about tempo, aggressiveness, speed, rhythm, and execution—the plays are just the stuff he uses to teach his players how to play with the kind of speed he wants. Malzahn's entire offense is built to be run without ever huddling, and at multiple speeds. Wherever he has been, Malzahn has taken a relentless approach to offense. And, for the players who get to showcase their talents in his up-tempo, hurry-up and go attack, it's relentlessly fun.

ODE TO THE WAR DADDIES:
TWO-GAP AND ONE-GAP DEFENSES—WHY NOT BOTH?

SPRING 2012

Football is a beautiful game. The NFL knows this. But how is the sport marketed? Mostly with quarterbacks. Maybe some receivers and a running back or two. But if fans watch the game to see men performing almost superhuman tasks, stuff that is like what most people can do but more kinetically gorgeous than anything we see in daily life, then I don't want to watch quarterbacks. Instead, I want to watch a three-hundred-pound man do things that no one should be able to do, typically to some other colossus who stands in his path; in short, I want to watch the New England Patriots' Vince Wilfork pulverize some other enormous human.

Here's an example. Late in the AFC championship game, the Baltimore Ravens trailed the New England Patriots 23–20, with the ball on the thirty-three-yard line and less than three minutes to play. It was fourth and six. Baltimore shifted into a four-wide receiver set, and the Patriots made a late adjustment to confuse the Ravens. After New England shifted its front, Baltimore's Pro Bowl center, Matt Birk, was left one-on-one with Wilfork. Birk is six-foot-four and 310 pounds, and he had no chance. As soon as the ball was snapped, Wilfork had beaten Birk. He got underneath Birk—Wilfork's arms were firmly planted on Birk's chest while Birk flailed his arms to try to regain some semblance of leverage. With his back flat and leaning forward, Wilfork drove Birk backward; in coach patois, he put Birk on "roller skates" and slid him directly into Ravens quarterback Joe Flacco. Wilfork eventually grabbed Flacco's jersey, forcing a desperate heave out of bounds, but as much as anyone else it was Birk, driven backward by Wilfork, who disrupted the play and sent the Baltimore offense off the field. Wilfork, through force, speed, and technique, had turned Birk into another New England defender. Such performances are beauty and truth, all in one 325-pound package.

Despite these moments of mastery, the Patriots' defense has not been very good this season. The statistics are ugly, and the defenders themselves are a motley group of undrafted rookies, castaways, and converted wide receivers. But no team wins a Super Bowl in today's salary cap–limited NFL by assembling a perfect roster. What New England coach Bill Belichick has is a jumble of defenders with varying skill sets who are all anchored by one immovable object: Wilfork. And good coaching is about making the most of what you have.

Aside from discussions of its general mediocrity (or worse), the hottest topic about the Patriots' defense has been how hard it is to define. Is it a 3–4 defense (the three defensive linemen, four linebacker defense that Belichick has run for two decades)? Or is it a 4–3 (the four defensive linemen, three linebacker set that New England has favored this year)? The truth is that they play a bit of both.

Then again, simple labels like 4–3 and 3–4 don't tell the full story. These 4–3 and 3–4 teams typically differ in a key respect: which technique their defensive linemen use. Usually, teams must commit to one technique or the other, as each choice has all sorts of other implications for the defense. It's truly a philosophical choice. Yet Belichick and his vagabond defenders have found a way to get the best of both worlds (relatively speaking) to best fit the Patriots' strengths. To understand Belichick's strategy, we have to understand how these techniques have evolved over time.

Playing defensive line is all about technique (although it doesn't hurt to be enormous and incredibly athletic). But it's about more than just large men pushing each other around. A defensive lineman must always be in the right position. Big running plays don't happen simply because one team wanted it more or because they knocked the other guy off the ball. It's all about angles and leverage, along with the technical savvy that makes the difference between a stuffed run and a fifty-yard touchdown. And the first question for a defensive lineman is always, Am I playing a two-gap technique or a one-gap technique?

"Gap" refers to the area between offensive linemen. A one-gap technique is just what it sounds like: the defensive lineman lines up in front of the gap he is responsible for, and his job is to attack and control it. If nothing else, a defender must not allow a runner to go through his gap. While defensive linemen attack their gaps, the linebackers behind them are responsible for their own gaps. These are the defense's "run fits," meaning how they fit into an offense's blocking scheme to take away running space.

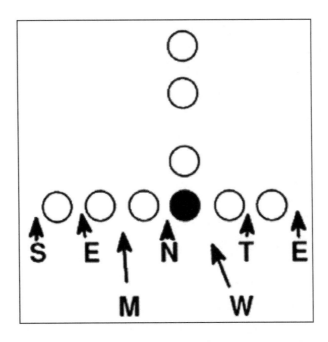

The two-gap technique, by contrast, sounds physically impossible. How can one player occupy two separate gaps? He does it by controlling the blocker. At the snap of the football, a two-gapping defensive lineman does what Wilfork did to Birk. He leads with his hands, gets leverage on the offensive lineman, and takes control of the blocker. From there, the advanced techniques kick in. On run plays, the defender reacts to where the blocker tries to take him. If he is double-teamed, he'll try to split the blockers and either shoot into the backfield or occupy the blockers, thus freeing up his teammates to make tackles.

In short, while a one-gap player attacks gaps, a two-gap player attacks people. Football's conventional wisdom states that an effective two-gap lineman, particularly one who lines up in the middle of the defense like Wilfork does, must be enormous. Coaches refer to them as "war daddies." But size is actually less important than athleticism and smarts. The line between touchdowns and stops in the NFL is exceedingly thin, and it's footwork and feel that are the difference. It is the most violent, most complicated, and most beautiful ballet I can think of.

So how did these techniques develop and evolve? In the early days of football, essentially everyone used a two-gap approach. It was all about beating blockers. One-gap techniques existed in blitz schemes where defenders were sent to specific spots, but as a general matter almost all defensive fronts for the premodern era of football relied on some kind of two-gap concept.

This trend became more entrenched around 1940, when T formation offenses came into vogue. These offenses were among the first to organize players in the way familiar to us now. Before them, most teams used shotgun-based offenses with multiple backs in the backfield, any one of whom might run, block, or even pass. Often, the halfback was the leading passer.

The T formation put the quarterback under center while others in the backfield ran in all directions. It was misdirection and confusion for the defense. And its most famous game was the 1940 NFL Championship, when Bears coach George Halas unveiled it against the Redskins, who had defeated them just a few weeks earlier. The result was different this time, as the Bears nuked the 'Skins 73–0 and Washington had no answers for Halas's new attack.

Defenses needed an answer. The response was the 5–2 Monster defense, which essentially dominated football for the next two decades. The 5–2 Monster involved five defensive linemen, each playing a two-gap technique over a specific offensive lineman. This allowed linebackers to roam free and match the offense's ball carriers. The "Monster" referred to the safety who came down and created one of the first true eight-man-front defenses. The combination of five two-gapping defensive linemen with three second-level defenders, each attacking the ball and following the potential runners, helped counteract the T formation offenses' misdirection.

In the NFL, defenses varied more owing to the need to stop passing teams, but even those variations typically relied on Monster-based principles. But eventually, this approach was forced out by the wishbone, triple option offense. The wishbone never took hold in the NFL, but that doesn't mean its effects weren't felt there, albeit indirectly.

The 5–2 Monster and its related defenses couldn't handle the wishbone. Great wishbone teams, beginning with coach Emory Bellard's University of Texas squads, began decimating defenses. In 1971, Oklahoma averaged over 470 yards rushing per game with the wishbone, a record that stands to this day. By not blocking some of the Monster's two-gap defenders to instead option off them, wishbone teams could trick the defense every time. A two-gap lineman can't control the blocker if the blocker doesn't engage with him at all. And because the offense chose not to block certain people, it had a numbers advantage against the rest of the defense. The 5–2 was outleveraged and outnumbered against the triple option.

But the story of football schemes is always one of punch-counterpunch, and the wishbone helped usher in the modern NFL defense. In 1979, Oklahoma State, a team whose schedule was perennially loaded with great wishbone teams, hired a defensive-minded coach named Jimmy Johnson. Among his various stops in college football, Johnson had served as defensive line coach at Oklahoma. He was even there during 1971, where he faced that record-setting rush attack in practice. Johnson saw every day how much trouble his defenders had with the triple option, given the Monster concepts he'd been teaching them.

Johnson's response was to reinvent the 4–3 defense with an almost entirely new underlying framework. And although this new 4–3 began at Oklahoma State, it is now known for the school Johnson brought it to next: the University of Miami. The 4–3 had been around for a long time. Legendary Dallas Cowboys coach Tom Landry even had his own variant named after him, the Landry 4–3 Flex, but Johnson concocted his version as anti-wishbone medicine. Instead of telling defensive linemen to two-gap and watching them get fooled by the option on every play, he switched entirely to a one-gap system. Johnson simplified things for them by giving them one job and telling them to attack. We still see this principle now; Detroit Lions coach Jim Schwartz, himself a former 4–3 defensive line coach, only slightly exaggerated when he said his playbook for defensive tackles consists of two words: "Kick butt."

In Johnson's Miami 4–3, aggressiveness, playing your assignment, and, above all else, speed, ruled. He famously made linebackers out of safety recruits and defensive ends out of linebacker recruits. His one-gap scheme allowed him to use smaller, faster, more athletic players. Johnson also lined his cornerbacks up near the line of scrimmage so they would be available to stop outside runs, while the safeties aligned deep. All together, Johnson's defense was sound against the wishbone. The middle linebacker covered the infamous fullback dive up the middle, while the other defenders—the defensive end, outside linebacker, safety, and cornerback—could account for the quarterback and pitch running back. Nowadays, whenever you see a defense smother a poorly run speed option on the sideline, you're seeing Johnson's principles at work.

But then a funny thing happened. It turned out that Johnson's 4–3 defense, designed to stop the wishbone (a so-called college offense), was extremely effective against almost everything, including NFL offenses. Johnson proved this by winning a couple of Super Bowls as head coach of the Dallas Cowboys using the same Miami 4–3. Johnson's one-gap approach was so effective it almost completely took over the NFL within just a few years. In fact, all of the Tampa Two defenses that later became popular were directly derived from the Miami 4–3.

Such trends are always easier to see in the past. Here in the present, amid various strategic schemes and approaches—3–4, 4–3, one-gap, two-gap, spread offense, pro-style, and so on—the trends swirl about and collide without any discernable pattern. In recent years, defenses have undergone radical changes and even have come back to the two-gap (and even one-gap) 3–4 schemes. Meanwhile, offenses have gotten more varied and spread than ever. Right now, there is no clear-cut favorite between two-gap and one-gap approaches. One-gap defenses keep schemes simple, but in a world of wide-open offenses, the two-gap approach allows defenses to keep extra players in coverage and to blitz from unexpected spots. We see lots of different defensive systems in the NFL right now because schemes in general are in flux.

This is precisely the atmosphere in which Bill Belichick thrives; he's comfortable amid shifting ideological currents. In addition to being a veteran defensive coach, Belichick is known as something of a football historian. His father coached for a very long time, including roughly four decades at the Naval Academy. Belichick grew up around football coaches, and he has witnessed this strategic evolution.

So what has Belichick done with his oddball assortment of defenders, anchored by Vince Wilfork? Did he choose 3–4 or 4–3? One-gap or two-gap? Traditionally a 3–4 coach, Belichick ran this system even when almost every other NFL team was mimicking the 4–3 defenses popular in Dallas and Tampa. But Belichick now finds himself in a time when, by desire and necessity, he has largely moved to a four-man line. And yet, in typical Belichick fashion, he has chosen not to rely solely on the 4–3 or 3–4 or a one-gap or two-gap approach. Nor does he just alternate between 3–4 and 4–3 looks from play to play. Instead, Belichick has essentially combined both approaches in the same play. How?

The Patriots run a 3–4 to one side of the field and a 4–3 to the other, all on the same play. The key to all this is Wilfork. He lines up over the center and assumes his traditional spot of run-stuffing, blocker-consuming, two-gapping war daddy. Belichick fills out the rest of the pieces based on the strengths and weaknesses of his other defenders.

In the traditional 4–3, there are two basic fronts: over and under. In Belichick's hybrid 4–3 over, Wilfork is responsible for controlling (that is, destroying) the center and thus the gaps to either side of him. To Wilfork's left, the defense functions just like a regular one-gap 4–3 scheme, with the other defensive tackle attacking the gap between guard and tackle and the defensive end covering the tight end. The strong side linebacker aligns to this side, and there will often be further run support, either from a safety or a cornerback. To the other side, however, it's all 3–4. The defensive end to Wilfork's right is a two-gap player, and there are two linebackers to that side as well, lined up as they would be in a traditional 3–4.

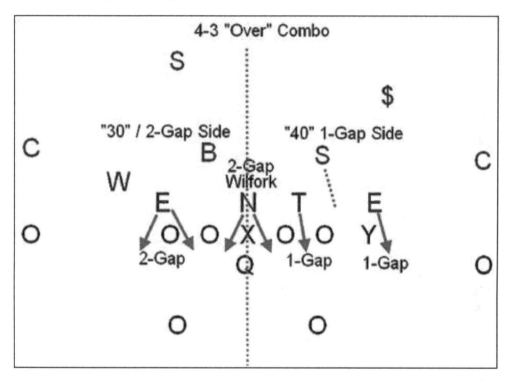

The traditional 4–3 under, which Monte Kiffin made famous with the Tampa Bay Buccaneers, has the defensive line slide away from the tight end while the strong side linebacker lines up facing the tight end on the line of scrimmage. This gives them something of a five-man front, in a nod to the old 5–2 Monster. Belichick's version is no different, except he again uses Wilfork to anchor the defense as a true two-gap player in the middle. This time, the 3–4 side is to Wilfork's left, toward the tight end, and the 4–3, one-gap side is to Wilfork's right.

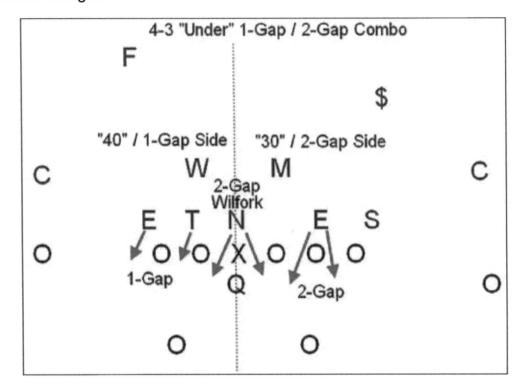

By combining these techniques into one defense, Belichick achieves what seems most important to him these days—versatility. He's able to plug different guys into different spots while knowing he has Wilfork anchoring the middle. As NFL offenses have become more and more spread, Belichick's defenses have become more versatile. With one or two players two-gapping on a given play, the outside linebackers in particular are free to blitz, drop into coverage, and attack running backs all over the field. Belichick rarely lets his scheme turn into a true 4–3; more often, he'll use the same assignments for each defender but use 3–4 personnel. The variations are endless. And it all works because Wilfork is in the middle, dominating his gaps and putting his blocker on skates.

Of course, nothing Belichick does will transform the Patriots' defense into a great one; they don't have the talent. But coaching is about more than talent. It's about taking the talent that's available and giving it the best possible chance to succeed. And that's something Belichick does incredibly well. So while this New England team may never be known as a great, or even good, defense, they're hoping to be remembered as something much better: a Super Bowl–winning defense.

Final Words

A book's completion is a huge undertaking that needs the cooperation and assistance of many people. I am incredibly appreciative of all the people who have helped make this project possible as I think back on this journey.

I want to start by expressing my gratitude to my family, who have always been my biggest supporters. Even when writing was difficult, their unwavering love and support helped me to persevere.

Also deserving of recognition are my friends, who have been an endless source of support and inspiration for me as I've been writing. I am sincerely grateful to them for their enthusiasm and feedback, which have shaped my thoughts and my writing.

I also want to say how grateful I am for the life experiences that have influenced my writing. These experiences, whether through personal setbacks or triumphs, have given me a distinct viewpoint and have assisted me in creating a piece of work that is both honest and genuine.

Moreover, I am incredibly appreciative of all the people and institutions that have given me access to research resources, information, and data. Their assistance has been crucial to my ability to develop my ideas and write precisely and accurately.

The academic and professional networks that have helped me throughout my career are also appreciated. Their advice and mentorship have been crucial in fostering my development as a writer and a person.

Additionally, I appreciate my coworkers and collaborators who have offered me insightful criticism as I was writing and who have assisted me in honing my ideas.

Finally, I'd like to thank my readers for supporting my writing. They are the reason I do it. Your interest in and comments on my work have motivated me to keep writing and to pursue excellence in everything I do.

To sum up, writing a book is a group effort that necessitates the cooperation and input of numerous people. I am appreciative of the support I have received along the way from my friends, family, life experiences, personal knowledge, research, and readers. I appreciate you being a part of this journey with me, and I hope that this work will have an impact on you.

Elsieq U Galvans

Printed in Great Britain
by Amazon

27770403R00082